Michael James, an artist and quiltmaker, teaches quiltmaking in several Boston-area schools, including the DeCordova Museum in Lincoln, Massachusetts. In addition, he conducts workshops and lectures on quilt design throughout the United States and Canada. His work has been exhibited in solo as well as in group shows, among these the Young Americans exhibition at the Museum of Contemporary Crafts in New York City.

MICHAEL JAMES

The Quiltmaker's Handbook

A Guide to Design and Construction

A SPECTRUM BOOK

PRENTICE-HALL, INC., Englewood Cliffs, New Jersey 07632

Library of Congress Cataloging in Publication Data

JAMES, MICHAEL
    The quiltmaker's handbook.

    (The Creative handcrafts series)   (A Spectrum Book)
    Bibliography: p.
    1. Quilting.   I. Title.
TT835.J35   746.4'6   77-15592
ISBN 0-13-749416-5
ISBN 0-13-749408-4 pbk.

To Judy, and to our son, Trevor

Frontispiece: Detail, *Florescent Rag.*
Hand-appliquéd and quilted cotton,
48″ x 48″ (author, 1977)

Printed in the United States of America

10   9   8

PRENTICE-HALL INTERNATIONAL, INC., *London*
PRENTICE-HALL OF AUSTRALIA PTY. Limited, *Sydney*
PRENTICE-HALL OF CANADA, LTD., *Toronto*
PRENTICE-HALL OF INDIA PRIVATE LIMITED, *New Delhi*
PRENTICE-HALL OF JAPAN, INC., *Tokyo*
PRENTICE-HALL OF SOUTHEAST ASIA PTE. LTD., *Singapore*
WHITEHALL BOOKS LIMITED, *Wellington, New Zealand*

Contents

APPENDIXES

BIBLIOGRAPHY 140

Preface

This book has grown out of classes and workshops in quiltmaking and quilt design that I have taught at, among other places, the De-Cordova Museum School in Lincoln, Massachusetts, and the Massachusetts College of Art. Because I believe that competence (and ultimately, innovation) in any art or craft grows out of a solid background in its traditional techniques, I have concentrated on detailed explanations of the quiltmaking processes. These are directed to the novice, who may never have sewn a stitch in his or her life; to the practitioner who is seeking assistance in technical refinement; and to the instructor searching for a systematic approach to teaching quiltmaking.

Because I believe that the aesthetic development of any art or craft is dependent on original and highly personal responses to the design problem, I have chosen to illustrate the text with examples of work that represent that search for a new vision. I am confident that these will serve to inspire the beginner as well as the practicing quilt artist, the traditionalist as well as the futurist.

ix

The most exciting surface image does not make a good quilt of one that is otherwise poorly constructed. Conversely, the finest workmanship does nothing more to a mediocre design than emphasize its mediocrity. In any art, respect for the processes of the hand must coexist with respect for the processes of the mind.

Michael James
Somerset Village, Massachusetts

Credits

My deepest thanks to Jean Ray Laury, and to Beth and Jeffrey Gutcheon, for their initial encouragement and continued interest in this project.

To each of the artists who provided me the means to present their work here, I offer very sincere thanks. Their willingness to share, coupled with their patient replies to my inquiries, lightened the load considerably.

My wife, Judy James, helped directly with much of the technical photography and helped indirectly in many more ways than can be mentioned here.

I thank Stuart Darsch for competent, professional photo processing and printing.

Most importantly, I wish to thank my students, whose enthusiastic involvements in quiltmaking have served to deepen my own commitment to the art.

All illustrations and photographs are by the author unless otherwise indicated.

Appendix D, "On Color in Quilts," is a revision of an article previously published in *Quilter's Newsletter Magazine*. It is used by permission of *Quilter's Newsletter*.

1 Introduction

QUILTMAKING: A RECENT HISTORY

We have witnessed during the past two decades a phenomenal reinterest in the so-called handcrafts, perhaps because our swiftly changing society has insistently propelled us beyond the industrial age into the complexities and uncertainties of the supersonic, highly automated future. In response, we have sought concrete and tangible means to reaffirm our individualities and creative capabilities. We have turned to weaving and pottery, to jewelry and basketry and woodwork, in our search for some small measure of fulfillment and/or self-discovery.

As it did in the past, quiltmaking has come to serve these needs, and on a massive scale. The necessary tools are few and easily accessible. As a traditional by-product of home sewing, supplies for quiltmaking were generally inexpensive and quite readily available; and due to the unabated growth of the home sewing industry, this continues to be the case.

1

The situation today, however, does not quite parallel that of quiltmaking 100 or more years ago; for in our general recognition of quiltmaking as an *art* form, we have come to acknowledge its rightful place as one of many sophisticated modes of visual expression. The eighteenth and nineteenth century quiltmaker, with rare exception, conceived of her quilt as an essentially functional object. This response, in part conditioned by the sex-aligned chauvinisms of the male-dominated art establishment of the period, encouraged a persistently romantic view of quilts on the part of the quiltmaker as well as her audience. Due perhaps most strongly to the consciousness-raising women's movement, this narrow view has begun more recently to be overruled by an appreciation of quilts as important artistic statements.

The liberation of the quilt, so to speak, from functional restrictions imposed out of necessity in earlier times has also encouraged exploration of the form as a creative vehicle. The concept of the *wall quilt* has allowed the quilt to be seen as an end in itself, relieved of design restrictions imposed by the structure of the bed. True, quilts have long been exhibited in hanging displays, in fairs and in museums as well as in private collections; much of their graphic impact is lost, after all, when seen on a horizontal surface. But the relationship to the bed and bedroom, and hence the association of quiltmaking with domestic activities, was never out of mind.

Although the label *quilt* still implies the stitching through of the top, filling, and backing layers and refers to a more or less flat (or low-relief) object, that object is no longer necessarily square or rectangular. It may have multiple sides and corners or may be round or may have openings and closures or other incidental modifications dictated by artistic intent.

To be sure, the bed quilt itself will always offer a workable surface design format, for in the relationship of the parts of a given quilt design to the parts of the bed lie untold creative challenges. In the coexistence and mutual give-and-take of conventional and innovative quilt forms, however, lies the full flowering of the art.

A QUILTMAKER'S PERSONAL HISTORY

I am frequently asked, in workshops and at lectures and in the classroom, how I became interested in quiltmaking. I suspect that part of the reason behind the curiosity is that I am a man, professionally involved in what has heretofore been considered primarily a woman's art (and still is). Though men have always made quilts, their numbers have been small indeed by comparison to the numbers of women who have been involved. And artists both male and female, conditioned to see aesthetic worth in terms of "high" art forms (painting, sculpture, music, and so on), have been until recently quite hesitant in accepting quiltmaking as an equally meaningful mode of creative expression.

I remember having always felt a special attraction to fabric. I responded to its tactility, and to the appearance of different weaves and different fibers, and perhaps most of all to the visual appeal of lengths of colored yardage. In painting, I had worked with washes and stains of pigment on canvas, preserving the inherent texture of the support as an element of the final surface. The move to permanently precolored fabric, though quite casual at the time and brought about in response to the graphic immediacy of quilt block designs, appears in retrospect to have been a natural progression.

My initial fascination with the form was deepened by awareness of the complete interdependence struck between good design and good workmanship in a successful final product. The sewing processes, then, did not become boring or tedious. On the contrary, each stitch took on a singular importance, and the rhythmic repetition of the same stitching motions afforded a vehicle by which full concentration could be given to the work at hand and to the piece as a whole.

My initial explorations of the medium revolved around the making of countless copies of traditional blocks as well as several small quilts in traditional patterns and finally two large, traditional quilts. Since that "apprenticeship," I have concentrated on working my own images, some quite closely related to traditional forms, others less so. In all of these, new technical challenges imposed by different design considerations create for me a vital interchange between craft and art.

The hand techniques that I describe and recommend in this book are those that I have used extensively in my own work. They are for the most part sewing processes that I developed as I searched for techniques that would take the least amount of time but would provide the strongest construction. This is not to say that they are original techniques, as I'm sure they are not (though they do seem to be "natural" ways of sewing). Nor is it to say that they are the fastest, since, quite certainly, the sewing machine can reduce the time needed dramatically. I feel confident, however, that when one chooses to work by hand, these methods will produce durable and long-lasting pieces.

This book is a manual of instruction. It sets the scene for an understanding of quilt design and presents in detail step-by-step explanations of the various sewing techniques used in the art of quiltmaking.

The word *design* as used here refers to the formal ordering of the compositional elements of the two-dimensional quilt surface. These elements may include pattern, line, light and dark contrasts and interchanges, color harmonies and contrasts, and spatial interchanges and illusions. Each of these design elements, by itself, is worthy of extended study and as such can only be dealt with indirectly in these pages.

Quilt design has contributed to two-dimensional decoration much that is unique to the form. It has also borrowed extensively from design traditions in assorted decorative arts and from widely differing cultures. Other arts, likewise, have borrowed from quiltmaking. A great body of design has been created, and it serves as a record of the historical development of the art. A limited number of familiar, pieced-quilt designs are presented within. It is my intention that they be used as vehicles for understanding how quiltmakers of the past oriented themselves to the pieced or appliqué or whole-cloth surface. For the beginner, these patterns can also be employed as convenient devices for learning the sewing techniques. At the start, the problem of learning how to sew well need not be complicated by the problem of designing original works of art.

Yet one reaches a point where familiarity with and/or mastery of the techniques begins to be wasted on uninspired copying of traditional patterns. It is here that the quiltmaker must begin to explore his or her own personal orientations to the design forms. The grid systems discussed in this book will assist you in making the transition from the conventional, anonymous image to one that is more personally expressive. This is not to say, however, that you must abandon the conventional block or set or border forms. To the contrary, having based your development on a careful study and understanding of the traditional surface, you will be better able to adapt and alter and reinterpret the familiar in creative ways and perhaps ultimately to make your own original contributions to the art.

Each of the traditional sewing techniques is dealt with under the corresponding design classification. The novice or student quiltmaker should work several small "samplers" in each method until a basic competence is developed. This can only be determined by comparison with skillfully worked models, but the examples used to illustrate the techniques should give a fair indication of the desired results. As soon as sewing appears to produce a fairly durable product, the student should begin work on a small quilt (suggested maximum size: 54 in. or 140 cm in any dimension). This first project should be designed to acquaint the quiltmaker with the processes of constructing the textile sandwich and should introduce an appreciation of the discipline, both technical and intellectual, needed to carry the work through to completion. It is important that the first quilt not be too large. The satisfaction experienced in sewing the final binding stitches on a quilt is always a strong incitement to further exploration of the medium. Too many would-be quiltmakers, overwhelmed by the "king-size" dimensions of their first eagerly begun quilt project, never experience that final satisfaction.

MCKAIN 1976

2 Materials

Quilts, being textile objects, are by nature fragile. As with most textiles, they can easily be affected by the adverse effects of strong light, temperature and humidity changes, dust, moisture, and general wear. Gradual, long-term deterioration due to all or some of these factors is not uncommon even with quilts that have lain unused or carefully stored for generations. Quiltmakers of the past often used whatever materials were at hand, from old clothing for the tops, to blankets for the batts, to flour sacks for the backings. It is little wonder that so few of the great number of quilts made during the past three centuries in this country have survived intact.

Contemporary quiltmakers should be concerned with the quality of the materials that go into making a quilt; and whenever possible, every effort should be made to obtain the best that one can afford.

FABRIC

It should first be said that the choice of fabric for a quilt will depend greatly on the design, manner of construction, and the intended function of the piece. In working a quilt entirely by hand, for instance, lightweight fabric—specifically 100 percent cotton broadcloth—will be most easily handled and will offer the least resistance to the hand-guided needle. A sheer gauze or voile that would be totally inappropriate for a bed quilt might be successfully employed for effect in a quilt that is to hang on a wall or under glass and receive little wear. A tightly woven percale or a heavy cotton duck might work well in a machine-pieced and -quilted project but would present an obstacle to the hand sewer.

One should consult a fabric guide (several manuals are available) to determine the characteristics of any fiber, either natural or man made, with which one is unfamiliar. Testing before use is also recommended. Will it shrink? All-cotton fabrics do tend to shrink and should be washed and dried to assure the maximum shrinkage at the outset. Does the fabric color run? A fabric may not bleed in warm water but may do so in hot. A safe rule is to wash a finished quilt in the same temperature water in which the quilt fabric was preshrunk. What is the fabric's "pressability?" A synthetic fabric that may require a cool iron to prevent scorching should not be used with 100 percent cotton, which will require a hot iron to eliminate wrinkles. Can all of the fabrics be dry-cleaned, if water washing is ruled unsuitable for certain fabrics in the proposed piece?

All-cotton broadcloth has long been regarded as the most suitable fabric for most traditional pieced and appliqué quilts. It is easy to sew, both by hand and machine, and if of good quality will launder and wear well. It is highly recommended for beginners in the craft and will continue to serve equally well as an adaptable medium for quilt artists working with innovative imagery.

THREAD

Quilting thread, preferably 100 percent cotton, is recommended for hand piecing and appliqué, and all hand quilting. Several brands are available in a range of colors. Choice of thread color should depend on the predominant tonality of the fabrics to be used.

For machine piecing and appliqué, a cotton-covered polyester thread is suitable. Machine quilting, however, should be done with quilting thread.

Any strong thread that can stand up to repeated folding and unfolding of the fabric and to stretching in the quilting hoop may be used for basting. I generally use a quilting thread in a contrasting color.

NEEDLES

Experience with the various hand-sewing techniques will allow you to make the best determination as to which size needle offers you the most ease in handling.

For hand piecing and appliqué, *sharps* are used. These are long, slender needles onto which a series of stitches may be taken before the needle is drawn through. Size 8 is recommended. It should be noted that the higher the number, the smaller the needle. Thus, a 10 would be smaller than an 8, whereas a 7 would be larger. The tightness of the weave of a fabric may on occasion dictate the size needle you must use in hand sewing.

Hand quilting is done with *quilting* needles, sometimes called *betweens*. Here again, size 8 is recommended for most cotton quilts. Individuals with particularly small fingers may find that they are able to use a smaller needle, such as a 10, quite comfortably.

BATTING

The experienced quiltmaker knows that there is more to batting than simply a consideration as to how much quilting need be done with each type. Much of the beauty of a quilt depends on the harmony established between the patchwork design and the physical and visual texture of the quilting. Indeed, the whole-cloth quilt, for example, depends entirely on this definition of line and surface relief that results from sewing through the inner filling.

Most nineteenth and early twentieth century quilts enclose cotton battings. The quilting in these quilts generally appears subdued, with a characteristically soft, finely textured overall "patina." Cotton battings are available today in sheet form, in several sizes, and should be handled with care in sandwiching it between the top and backing. Once basted in, however, the quilt may be placed in and taken out of the hoop at will without disturbing the batt. Quilting must be fairly close; it is recommended that no space larger than 2 in. (5 cm) by 2 in. be left unquilted. It is in the nature of cotton batting to shift and bunch in washing when not quilted adequately.

Dacron battings have achieved a widespread popularity among quiltmakers during the past several decades, primarily because they need not be quilted as closely as cotton in order to launder well. It is characteristic of quilts with dacron batts that quilting lines appear much more strongly defined, and the overall quilting pattern appears to be in higher relief. Dacron batts vary greatly in quality from brand to brand, but as a general rule, only *bonded* battings should be used. These are battings that have been treated to promote ease in handling and to prevent the polyester fibers from penetrating the surface fabrics of the quilt. Particularly when used with cotton and polyester blend fabrics, the unbonded batts will lose fibers through the surface of the quilt, producing an undesirable "linty" coating.

The use of dacron batting allows the quiltmaker much more freedom in designing quilting patterns, as the restriction against larger, unquilted areas is removed. It also lends itself to textural variations and contrasts between closely quilted and open areas.

Wool batting, more common in this country before 1825, has qualities that merge both of the types above and thus deserves the attention of the serious quiltmaker. Though it requires close quilting as with cotton batting, it has the springiness and "height" of dacron and thus produces a strongly defined quilting design. It is not, however, widely available commercially, and to prepare one from scratch is a major undertaking in itself.

The quiltmaker should work projects with each of the two major types of batting to evaluate the characteristics of each and thus to be better prepared to judge beforehand which type would lend itself best to a particular quilt project. The choice of batting should rest as much on the aesthetic demands of the project as on the time element involved in the quilting of each type.

THE HOOP

Historically, the quilting bee as a social institution was organized around the quilting frame, a wooden structure designed to hold the quilt taut during quilting. It was simply a large frame made of four

6 ft. (180 cm) to 10 ft. (300 cm) poles, held together at its corners with pegs or clamps and supported by its own stand or by the backs of wooden chairs. Anywhere from eight to sixteen quilters could be accommodated at one sitting.

As a means of getting the work done with friends and neighbors, the frame remains unchallenged as a functional apparatus. Not only does the frame support the entire quilt, but its cross-bars also provide a resting place for the quiltmaker's arm as he or she works. Spools of thread and scissors can rest on the surface close at hand.

The quilt frame, no matter how small, does occupy quite a bit of space, however; and so it is generally impractical for continued use in the home. Also, the quilt, once set in the frame, should remain there until finished; so this lack of portability presents another drawback.

A wooden quilting hoop will give equally fine results and has the obvious advantage of being both portable and space saving. The hoop should be round, about 23 in. (56 cm) in diameter, and should have wooden blocks on the outer hoop through which a long bolt is tightened. It can be supported during quilting on a table or chair; some models come with a stand to which the inner hoop may be attached. Oval hoops, which do not maintain an even tension across the stretched portion of the quilt, are not recommended.

Figure 2-1 *Tools for quilting.*

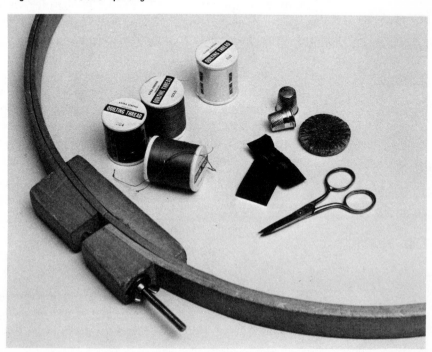

All of the author's quilts shown in this book were quilted on a round, wooden hoop of the type described.

In addition to the above, a few general tools are required.

Well-sharpened dressmaker's shears are necessary for cutting fabric, and they should be reserved for this purpose only. Embroidery scissors or a small pair of utility scissors should be used in cutting thread. Not only will this preserve the cutting edge of the shears, but the smaller scissors are by nature lightweight and more easily handled. An additional pair of scissors should be used in cutting paper or lightweight cardboard templates, although a razor-knife used to cut heavier cardboard templates may be used in this instance as well.

A cake of beeswax or a piece of paraffin should be used to wax thread for hand sewing. This helps to prevent knotting and strengthens the thread and also helps it to glide smoothly through the fabric.

Thimbles for quilting should fit the middle finger of the right hand and the index finger of the left, if one is right-handed. The reverse applies to the left-handed quilter. The thimbles should have a relatively flat face, with a well-defined top edge. Thimbles with rounded ends are unsuitable for the techniques described within, as are plastic thimbles.

A 24 in. (61 cm) metal or metal-edged ruler is practical for marking templates as well as for marking straight quilting patterns on the quilt top.

An *Exacto* or other razor-bladed knife will be necessary for cutting matboard or illustration board templates. The knife should have a narrow handle and should be held in the hand as one holds a pencil. Number 11 replacement blades are recommended for use with the Exacto.

Other materials are discussed within the relevant chapters. Individual preference for particular supplies and materials varies greatly from quiltmaker to quiltmaker. You should try a range of materials as the demand arises; what works well in one project may not in another. The necessity for fine quality in construction and workmanship should be the determining factor in regard to your choice of tools.

3 Pieced Work

Piecing is the seaming together of smaller units of fabric to form a larger whole. In the past, the term "patchwork" has been used to describe this same process; yet it has had a more general application as well in referring to appliqué processes. It is, more specifically, a reference to surface design. For our purposes, therefore, *piecing* and *pieced work* will be used as terms descriptive of the technical processes of seamed patchwork.

GEOMETRIC DESIGN

Shapes characteristic of pieced work are predominantly geometric in nature, as opposed to the organic or free-form figures of most appliqué work. The most widely used geometric shapes include squares, rectangles, triangles, diamonds, rhomboids, pentagons, hexagons, octagons, and parts of circles (i.e., quarter- or half-circles).

These shapes can be found singly or grouped together in the many hundreds of patterns that make up the bulk of traditional pieced-quilt designs.

In reproducing or adapting an antique pattern as well as in creating an original geometric design, it is helpful to understand the underlying grid structure on which a particular design is based. To this end, we'll take a look at two structural systems that can be used to facilitate duplication of traditional patterns as well as to create original designs. In beginning your exploration of pieced-work design, I suggest that you not only use the diagrams in this chapter as prepared models for planning quilt blocks, but that you also familiarize yourself with their construction by copying and enlarging them with ruler and pencil on either graph or drawing paper. Once you are able to do so accurately and to any dimension, you will be better prepared to adapt these and others or to draft new patterns.

GRID SYSTEM 1

The unifying factor for patterns developing out of this system is an underlying grid of equal units out of which the final block design is developed by further subdividing the units and then determining color combinations and contrasts. The quilt plan develops after a choice of the block pattern and in turn of a "set" for the quilt; that is, how the blocks are to be put together—with or without a lattice, or with alternate plain blocks, and so on (see Chap. 6).

Nine-patch (or three-patch) is perhaps the most familiar pieced-work grid. Nine equal squares are grouped together three-by-three

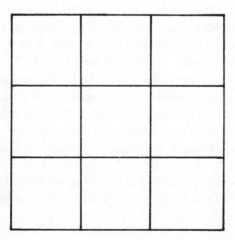

Figure 3-1 *Nine-patch* or three-patch.

Figure 3-2 *Nine-patch blocks.* a. Variable Star b. Hovering Hawks c. Quartered Star d. Double-T e. Crown of Thorns f. Corn and Beans

and subdivided to create the desired pattern. The dimensions of the individual square units, and consequently of the whole block, are freely variable depending on the desired visual effect. It may be suggested, as a general guideline, that the scale for basic grid designs be kept within a range of 10 in. (25.5 cm) to 20 in. (51 cm) when working with a traditional, repeated-block pattern. For example, the simple Variable Star pattern (Fig. 3-2a) will tend to create a livelier surface when the blocks are from 6 in. (15 cm) to 12 in. (30.5 cm) square, with individual units at 2, 3, or 4 in. (5 cm, 7.5 cm, 10 cm) square, respectively. It should be noted that a choice of scale that divides easily will simplify much of the business of drafting patterns and, later, templates. Keep in mind, nevertheless, that any selection of measurements for individual blocks within a chosen dimension for the quilt top will depend upon the desired visual impact and rests ultimately on your own creative judgment.

Four-patch grid patterns are made up of groupings of four units totaling sixteen squares. In some traditional patterns, such as Wind-

14

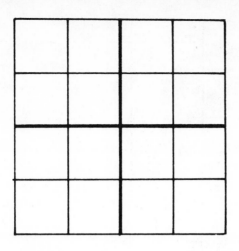

Figure 3-3   *Four-patch.*

Blown Square (Fig. 3-4b) and Sugar Cone (Fig. 3-4e), the repeat units are identical in layout of shapes, and each of the repeat units within the larger block design is based on its own four-patch grids. In others, such as Fireflies (Fig. 3-4c), two distinct repeat units are used within the grid.

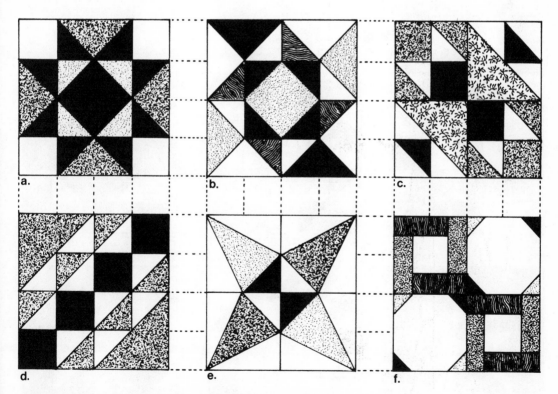

Figure 3-4   *Four-patch blocks.* a. Eight-Pointed Star b. Wind-Blown Square c. Fireflies d. Road to Heaven e. Sugar Cone f. Round the Twist

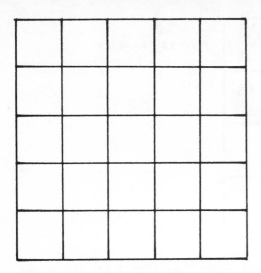

Figure 3-5   *Five-patch.*

Five-patch grid patterns are actually based on a grouping of twenty-five squares, five-by-five. In patterns such as Father's Choice and Jack-in-the-Box, the element of central crossing bands is emphasized, and in a block-to-block set these bands will join to give the effect of lattice.

Figure 3-6   *Five-patch blocks.* a. Father's Choice b. Square Dance c. Jack-in-the-Box d. Twister e. Sawtooth f. Flying Geese.

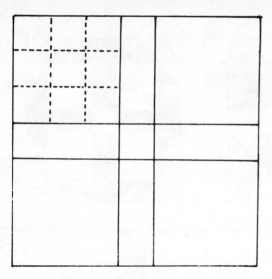

Figure 3-7 *Intersecting parallel lines.*

Intersecting parallel line blocks frequently bear strong resemblances to five-patch blocks. Their structure, however, is somewhat more complicated. Perhaps the simplest way to understand this grid is to outline on graph paper a block consisting of forty-nine squares, seven-by-seven. Now mark two sets of parallel lines running through the middle of the block from side to side and from top to bottom. The intersection of these parallel lines defines the center square. The four corner sections that result are basically nine-patch grids that are then subdivided to determine a particular pattern. The width of the space between either two sets of parallel lines is one-third the measurement of the corner (nine-patch) section. For example, if the space between the parallel lines is 2 in. (5 cm) in width, then the corner section will measure 6 in. (10 cm), and the full size of the block will be 14 in. (35.5 cm).

Diagonals that divide square units from corner to corner often function as foundation structures for pieced-work designs. Triangular units resulting from the diagonal cross are subdivided to create particular patterns, as in Figs. 3-8d through 3-8f.

These grid categories are presented here to simplify the matter of drafting traditional, pieced-work designs and their variations, as well as to help you to recognize exactly how a pieced pattern was constructed when you run across one in a quilt. Naturally, this ability to recognize the underlying components and structure of a given pattern in a quilt is something that develops only with practice and frequent study of quilts both old and new. Many patterns do not fall neatly into any one of these five categories, whereas others may fit into two grid categories simultaneously. Your experience with the grids presented here will help you to understand and to draft those also.

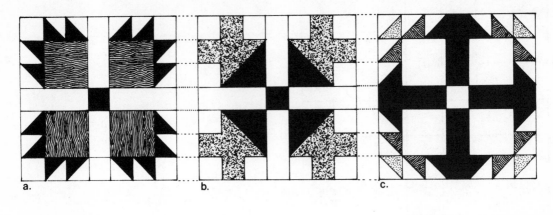
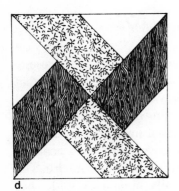
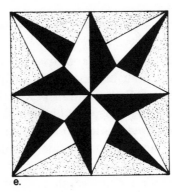
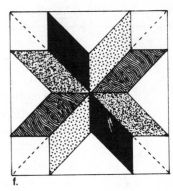

Figure 3-8 *Intersecting parallel line blocks and diagonal blocks.*
a. Bear's Tracks b. Lincoln's Platform c. Surprise Package
d. Windmill e. Western Star f. Eight-Pointed Star.

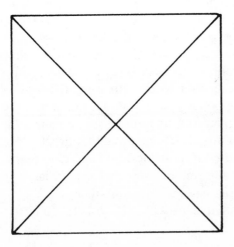

Figure 3-9   *Diagonal.*

18

A second system for designing geometric patterns is based on over-all grids of repeated units. The most common form of this type of grid is a sheet of graph paper, in which the individual unit is the square.

The obvious advantage of this form of grid system for the quilt-maker interested in developing original patterns is that it provides a basic groundwork within which one can freely adapt shape and tone contrasts in either a repeat or a random (abstract) pattern. The possibilities for variation are limitless, and the probability of spontaneous or accidental development of geometric surface designs affords a unique vehicle for creative expression.

Study the examples based on the three grids presented on the following pages. In working your own patterns, you may want to use the grids in the book by overlaying these with sheets of tracing paper on which you can pencil or color your designs. You may also enlarge the grids to scale on separate sheets of paper and use these as master sheets over which you may then work.

Grid pattern A is the standard graph paper form, here ruled with two line thicknesses to set off sixteen squares to the larger unit, or four squares to the inch. Many of the traditional pieced-block patterns previously discussed fit easily into this foundation.

Grid pattern B is made up of squares crossed corner-to-corner with diagonal lines. The feeling of motion implied by the contrasting linear directions helps to produce very active visual surfaces.

Grid pattern C uses identical rows of equilateral triangles. The familiar hexagon, block, and diamond patterns based on the 60-degree angle can be planned on this grid.

Each of these grids, and their variations, have been in use by artists, architects, and designers for centuries, and the decorative potential that each holds can yet be of service to the imaginative quiltmaker.

Figure 3-10a

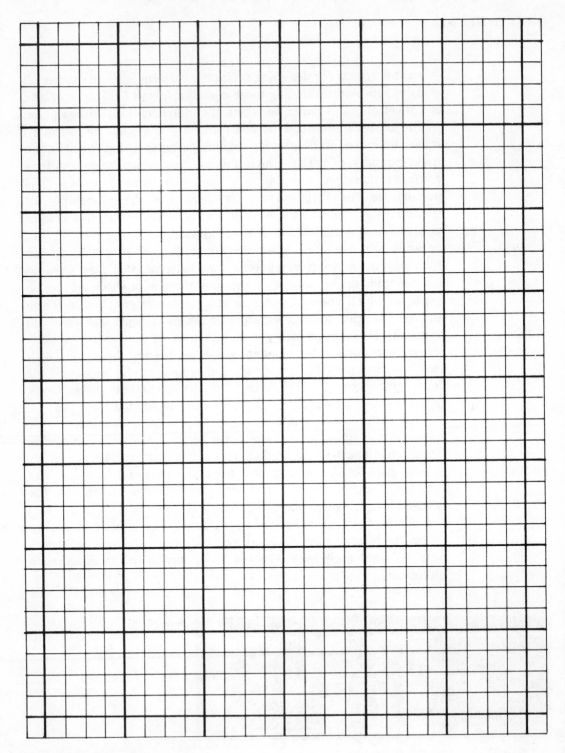

Figure 3-10 *Pattern A.* Square grid.

Figure 3-11 Block and border designs worked on square grid.

Figure 3-12 *Pattern B.* Crossed-square grid.

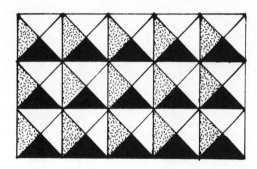

Figure 3-13 Designs worked on crossed-square grid.

Figure 3-14 *Pattern C.* Diamond grid.

Figure 3-15   Designs worked on diamond grid.

The adventure of making quilts, as with any process in which the designer is also the workman, is not without its more tedious aspects. I'm referring here to the business of drafting and cutting templates and marking and cutting fabric. Many quiltmakers (myself included) tend to look at these processes as obstacles to the more satisfying work of putting the pieces together. Nevertheless, the correct fit of all the fabric pieces and the eventual accurate "finish" of the whole top are highly dependent on the precision with which templates and fabric are marked and cut.

Templates are the pattern pieces for each shape in a given design. There are many ways to prepare templates, as many as there are materials out of which to make them. I have preferred the use of single-thickness cardboard, specifically designer's illustration board. I have found this material to be durable, readily available, and easily handled. For large-scale quilt projects involving hundreds of pieces, a double-thickness illustration board (about ⅛ in. [3 mm] thick) has proven best in holding sharp edges and points. For small projects such as pillows and crib quilts, one may be tempted to use poster board, which can be cut with scissors, but the very short life of such templates makes use of the material impractical.

Over-all patterns using only one shape will usually require but one template. This should be marked with scrupulous accuracy. The slightest variation in measurement between any two or more adjoining sides of pattern pieces will affect the "fit" of the entire surface. Inexpensive plastic triangles available in stationery or art supply shops can facilitate the drafting of squares, rectangles, and triangles, although with care these may be drawn with ruler alone. A compass will be needed to draft equilateral triangles, hexagons, and diamonds.

To draw a triangle with three equal sides, first determine the length of each side; this may be any measurement you wish to work with. Rule a line A to correspond to the desired length—say, 3 in. (7.5 cm)—and open the compass to that same measurement. Place the metal point of the compass at one end of the ruled line, and describe an arc upward from the line. Repeat this step at the other end of the line. The point where the two arcs intersect will define the third point of the triangle, and each of the three sides should be exactly the same measurement.

The hexagon is easily drawn by first marking a circle with the compass. Without changing the opening of the compass (which is the radius of the circle), place the metal point anywhere on the

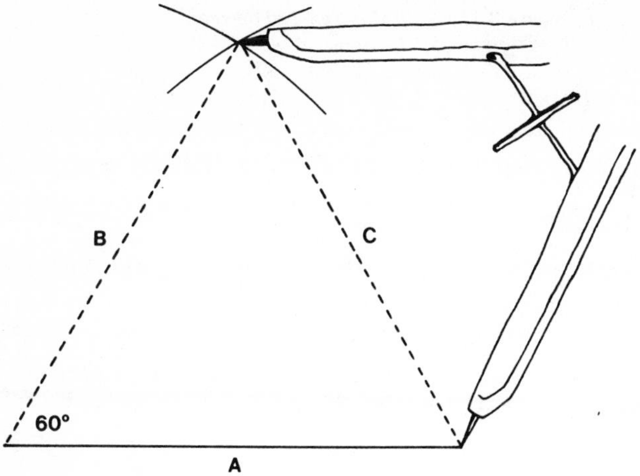

Figure 3-16 *Drafting equilateral triangle.*

circumference and begin describing arcs that will intersect the circle at equal intervals. Note that the compass is moved after each arc is drawn, and the metal point placed on the point where the arc crosses the circle. Straight lines are ruled between each of the six intersecting arcs, and a hexagon results.

Diamonds for the six-pointed star as well as for the "Tumbling Block" or cube patterns are based on the hexagon. Draft a hexagon as described above. To form the 60-degree-120-degree diamond, rule lines between opposite points so that two lines cross at the center of the hexagon. The diamond results, as well as corresponding equilateral triangles.

Figure 3-17a *Drafting hexagon.*

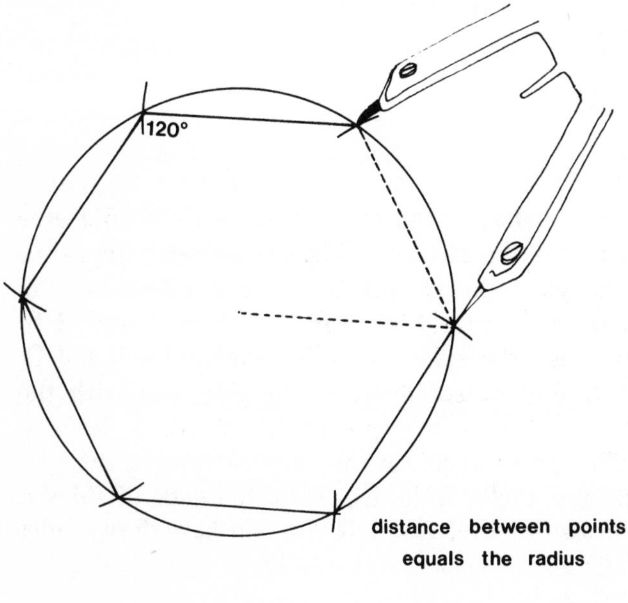

distance between points
equals the radius

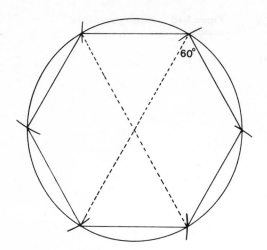

Figure 3-17b *Drafting 60-120-degree diamond.*

Remember that a diamond has four equal sides—not to be confused with a rhomboid, whose opposite sides only are equal. This is a common point of confusion, particularly when drafting eight-pointed star patterns and their variations. Rhomboids are easily drawn within rectangles on any of the grids previously mentioned and will produce an elongated star if used for that pattern (see Fig. 3-8f).

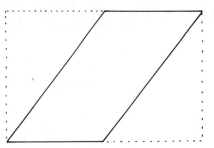

Figure 3-18 *A rhomboid.*

The diamond for the eight-pointed star is based on the 45-degree angle. To draft it, first mark a 45-degree angle, either with the aid of a plastic or metal triangle or by drawing a square and dividing it in half on the diagonal, as in Fig. 3-19. Mark off sides A and B to whatever length you wish the sides to be. To mark sides C and D, open the compass to the measurement of the side; and with the metal point placed alternately at the ends of lines A and B, describe arcs that intersect. The point at which they intersect marks the base of the second 45-degree angle. Rule lines from the ends of sides A and B to the intersection of the arcs, and you will have drawn sides

C and D.

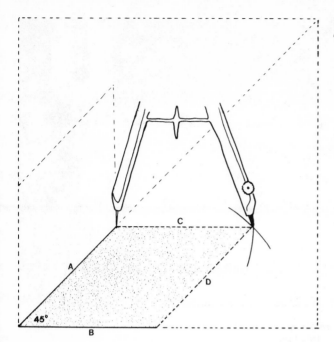

Figure 3-19 *Drafting 45-135-degree diamond.*

With patterns consisting of more than one shape, first determine exactly how many shapes are in the block or repeat. The size you choose for the block will determine the size of each respective shape. For example, the nine-patch block pattern Double-T (Fig. 3-2d) contains three sizes of triangles and a square, for a total of four template pieces. The five-patch Square Dance (Fig. 3-6b) employs three template shapes—a square, a triangle, and a trapezoid. The block Western Star (Fig. 3-8e) is made up of three triangular templates. To assure accuracy of measure and fit of all template shapes in a design, it is helpful to draft to size on cardboard the entire block or that portion thereof that contains at least one of each of the shapes (see Fig. 3-20). In this way you will be assured beforehand of the likelihood that all of your fabric pieces will fit together.

For hand sewing, templates are cut to correspond to the finished size of the fabric piece; they *do not* include seam allowance. To prepare the templates, first mark each shape as accurately as possible on the cardboard (see Fig. 3-20). With lightweight material such as posterboard, you may then cut the pieces with scissors. With the heavier illustration boards, the neatest edge and point finish will be achieved with the use of an *Exacto* or other razor-bladed utility knife and a metal or metal-edged ruler. Place the ruler so that it is aligned with the penciled edge of the shape you wish to cut. Hold the ruler firmly in place so that it will not slip, and with the other hand draw the point of the blade along the edge of the ruler in a

Figure 3-20 *Cutting templates.* Note that knife blade is held perpendicular to metal edge of ruler.

steady, continuous motion. Do not try to cut through the board in one pass, but repeat the motion until you have made a clean, gradual cut through the entire thickness. Take care to hold the knife so that the blade is perpendicular to the template and to the ruler during the cutting. If the knife is held at an angle, the resulting template could be slightly larger than the desired measurement, and your fabric pieces would not fit together properly. Use of the knife assures crisp edges and points. Remember when cutting with razor knives to place your work on a surface that won't damage or be damaged by the cutting blade. Homesote (from a lumber yard), several thicknesses of newspaper, or old magazines work well.

For machine sewing, templates are made to include the ¼-in. (6-mm) seam allowance. A line is ruled parallel to and ¼ in. (6 mm) from the straight edge of the board. The shape of the template representing the finished size of the piece is outlined, using part of the ruled parallel line as one side of the piece. These lines correspond to the sewing lines. Seam allowances for the remaining sides are then marked by measuring a series of dots ¼ in. (6 mm) from each line and then connecting these dots to determine the final size of the template. These cutting lines may also be marked with the aid of a clear plastic dressmaker's T-square ruled with a ⅛-in. grid. The ¼-in. seam allowance is added along each side by aligning the ¼-in. mark on the ruler with the outline of the shape, as in Fig. 3-21.

Figure 3-21 *Drafting templates for machine sewing.* Inner line of
each template piece is *sewing* line.

The necessity for accurate measurement cannot be stressed too
strongly. All template shapes for a given design must fit together
precisely. A difference in size of adjoining pieces, however slight,
will affect the ultimate fit and measure of the entire piece of work.

Instructions on determining the number of template and fabric
pieces for a large project and on estimating yardage can be found
in Chap. 6.

MARKING THE FABRIC

Here again, accuracy is very important. Careless marking, no matter
how accurate the templates, can easily result in a misshapen-pieced
project.

Shapes for pieced work are marked on the *wrong* side of the
fabric. For hand sewing, templates are spaced approximately $1/2$ in.
(1.3 cm.) apart, thus providing a $1/4$-in. (6-mm) seam allowance for
each fabric piece once the shapes are cut, as in Fig. 3-22. The marked
line is the sewing line. The spacing of the templates may be done by
eye, providing that rows of shapes are marked in a uniform and
orderly fashion, thus eliminating waste (see Fig. 3-24).

Figure 3-22   *Marking fabric for hand sewing.*

For machine sewing, the template is placed so that its edge is aligned with the edge of the previously marked piece. The marked line in this case is the cutting line.

All marking of shapes should be done with a number two pencil, which should be sharpened frequently to maintain as sharp a point

Figure 3-23   *Pieces marked for machine sewing.*

as possible. When working with darker fabrics on which pencil markings may be more difficult to see, a dressmaker's white chalk or artist's white drawing pencil may be used. It should be noted that it is very difficult to maintain a sharp point with the dressmaker's chalk pencil and that this also tends to rub off in working your pieces. A blunt or rounded end on the marking pencil can enlarge the size of each fabric piece by as much as ⅛ in (3 mm) all around. A fine point, on the other hand, assures a marking that will be closest to the actual size of the template.

Place templates on the fabric so that the maximum number of sides of each piece are on the straight of the fabric (Fig. 3-24). The *straight* grain of the woven fabric runs parallel to the selvages and has virtually no stretch. The *crossgrain*, involving the weft threads running perpendicular to the selvages, does stretch, but not substantially. The *bias* of the fabric runs diagonally to the straight and to the selvage and is the direction of maximum stretch of the fabric. Keeping bias sides to a minimum is one of the best assurances of accurate fit.

Preshrink and press all fabric before marking. To help prevent stretching of the fabric while marking, it is helpful to lay out the fabric on a surface covered with a flannel-backed tablecover—flannel

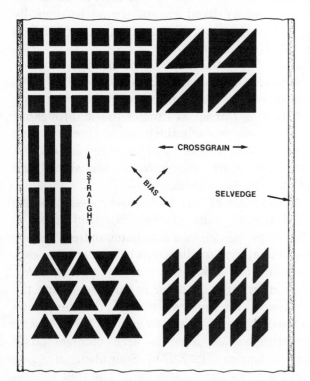

Figure 3-24 *Cutting layout for geometric shapes.*

side up—or with fabric-backed, vinyl upholstery—wrong side up—to which the fabric can cling. Hold the template firmly in place, and apply only enough pressure with the pencil to produce a crisp, visible line. Mark each side of the template in separate motions. Don't try to make one continuous marking all around the template, as the sharp point of the pencil can easily get caught in the threads and pull the fabric, thus distorting the shape.

Use dressmaker's shears to cut the fabric once the marking has been done. Cut each piece singly, and stack pieces according to color and shape.

SEWING

The quiltmaker's choice of piecing by hand or by machine should be made after experience with both techniques has defined the particular characteristics of each in terms of working time, strength, "finish" of the product relative to the amount of quilting to be done, and suitability to the execution of a particular design. It can't be denied that piecing by machine is faster and generally stronger than a hand running stitch, but it should also be kept in mind that everything that can be done by hand cannot always be done by machine. Therefore, it is important that the quiltmaker develop skill and accuracy with both techniques.

Hand-piecing tools are few and simple. For needles, number eight (8) sharps are standard. Thread may be a number fifty (50) standard weight cotton thread, or a cotton-covered polyester thread, or 100 percent cotton quilting thread, as I prefer to use throughout a hand-worked quilt. Since only a single thickness of thread is used in the actual sewing, the quilting thread provides added strength. A pair of embroidery or small utility scissors for cutting thread and a container of straight pins are also required.

The sequence of construction of any pieced-work design begins with the sewing of the smaller units of the design and grows to eventually make up the larger whole. In a nine-patch pattern such as "Jacob's Ladder" (Fig. 3-25a), five smaller units of four squares each are first sewn, along with four units each made of two triangles. These nine units are then arranged in order in three rows, and the units of each row are then sewn together. Finally, the three rows are joined along two parallel seams. In the four-patch "Dutchman's Puzzle," two smaller triangles are sewn to each of eight larger triangles, forming eight rectangles (Fig. 3-25b). Four identical square units are then constructed of two rectangles each. The four squares

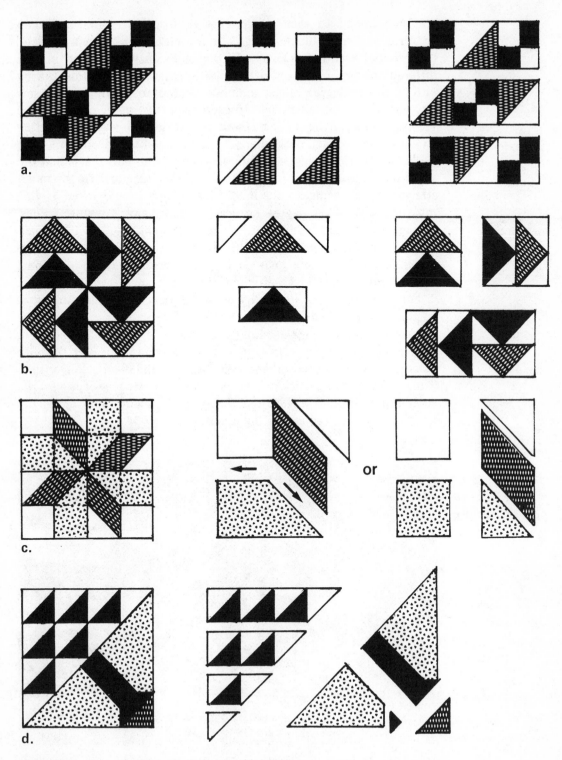

Figure 3-25 *Sequence of construction.* a. Jacob's Ladder
b. Dutchman's Puzzle c. Clay's Choice d. Pine Tree.

are then joined to each other, first to form two rows, and then to form the final block design. In the block for "Clay's Choice" (Fig. 3-25c) identical quarters of the block may be pieced in two different orders. Using only four pieces, construction entails sewing out of a 135-degree angle, a simple procedure providing you sew outward from the wide angle to each respective outer point. In the second method, the largest piece is divided in two, facilitating straight-seam piecing, particularly for working at the machine.

The main principle to keep in mind for any pieced work is that the sequence of construction should be ordered to allow for as much straight-seam piecing as possible. That is, one should avoid sewing into and out of 90-degree corners, or any similarly acute angles. Though this sewing would be more easily accomplished by hand than by machine, it is nevertheless an obstacle to precise construction. When such a situation is unavoidable, care should be taken in pinning and the sewing should be directed out of the angle, as in Fig. 3-25c.

Fabric pieces to be joined by hand are placed right sides together so that the penciled sewing lines are visible on both pieces. These markings must be aligned along the length of the side to be sewn, so a pin is first inserted through the corresponding point on both pieces where the seam will end (Fig. 3-26). If the seam is longer than 3 in. (7.5 cm) and particularly if the seam is on the bias of the fabric, several pins should be inserted through the sewing lines along the length of the seam to assure alignment.

Figure 3-26 *Preparation for hand piecing.* First pin is inserted at point where sewing will end.

A length of thread of from 12 in. (30.5 cm) to 18 in. (46 cm) is practical for hand piecing. Lengths in excess of 18 in. (46 cm) easily twist and knot during the sewing and will begin to wear as the sewing progresses. Knot the end of the thread at the point where it is cut as it comes off the spool.

Begin sewing by inserting the threaded sharp through the corresponding points at the beginning of the penciled seam line, thus aligning these points in the same manner as the end that has been pinned. Proceed with a running stitch as shown in Figs. 3-27 through 3-30. The needle should be guided with the thumb and index finger of the sewing hand so that the point moves back and forth between the two thicknesses of fabric to form tiny, uniform stitches. The other hand holds the fabric pieces together and moves them toward you, then away from you as you push the needle, thus affording a clear view of the penciled line on both pieces of fabric. As the needle is manipulated along the seam line, it is "loaded" with fabric; and anywhere from four to twelve stitches may be taken—depending on the thickness of the fabric—before the needle and thread are drawn through. Remove pins as the sewing proceeds (Fig. 3-29).

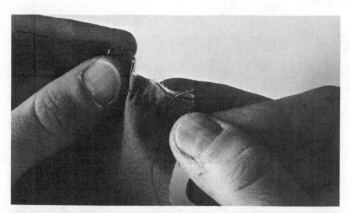

Figure 3-27   Sewing hand guides needle as other hand moves fabric back and forth onto needle.

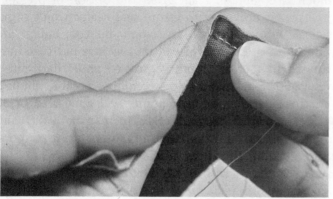

Figure 3-28   Sewing must correspond to pencil lines on both fabric pieces.

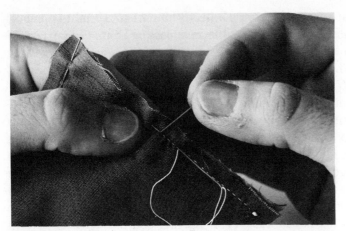

Figure 3-29   Pin removed as needle passes.

Figure 3-30   Thread knotted by guiding needle through loop formed with backstitch at end of line.

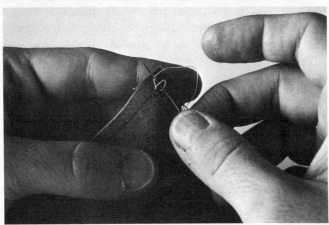

End a row of stitching with either a knot or several backstitches (Fig. 3-30). I prefer not to sew through seam allowances to the raw edge of the fabric; I knot off all hand-pieced seams at the end of the penciled line. As I usually reserve any pressing of hand-pieced work until a block is complete, I am given the option of pressing in whichever direction is necessary to assure that seams won't show through lightweight fabrics and points won't be too bulky. If, however, you choose to press each pieced unit as it is put together, keep in mind that light fabrics should be pressed *under* dark ones.

Joining rows together within a block requires precise pinning where seams are to be joined so that points will appear to meet accurately on the right side of the work. This can be a difficult problem to resolve in hand piecing, especially when eight or more pieces of fabric are intended to meet at a fine point.

The process of joining rows with cross-seams is shown in Fig. 3-31. First, align the rows with right sides together, and pin through corresponding points where the sewing will end. Working backward from this last pin, join any seams that must meet by pinning through at corresponding points on the pencil lines. It is helpful to allow the pin to catch a thread or two of each fabric piece that is to meet at the point, first piercing each of the pieces in one row, then each of the corresponding pieces in the other. Set the pin down into the fabric, perpendicular to the seam you are going to sew. As the sewing begins and proceeds, remove each pin as a stitch is about to be taken over it, being careful that the seams being joined meet as this is done. Where six or more pieces of fabric are to meet, it will be necessary to avoid sewing down the seam allowances when joining the rows, as the thickness of multiple seam allowances at a point is difficult to pierce properly with a hand running stitch. In such cases, sew only through the two matched pencil lines. For simple cross-seams involving three or four pieces at a point, the seam allowance may be pressed to one side (light under dark, whenever possible) and sewn down, providing this thickness does not interfere with the size and uniformity of the running stitch.

Figure 3-31 *Pinning and joining cross-seams.*

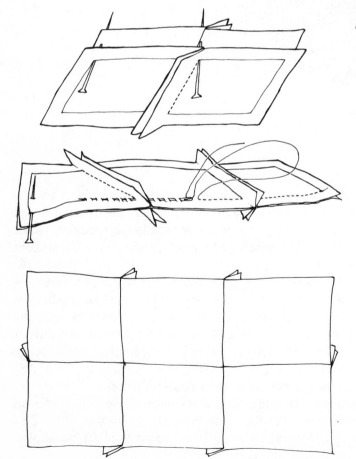

When a block is complete, press the seam allowances to one side as neatly and uniformly as possible, first from the wrong side of the block and then from the right side, using a pressing cloth (a piece of muslin works fine) to prevent the iron from glazing the fabric. Figure 3-32 shows the back of a neatly pressed, pieced block.

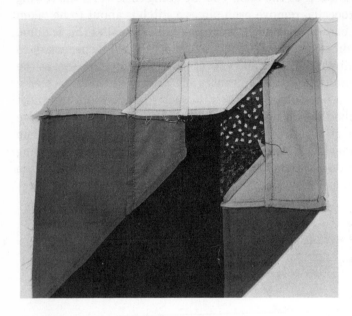

Figure 3-32 *Completed block.* Hand-pieced block properly pressed.

MACHINE PIECING

Cotton-covered polyester thread works well for machine piecing and is recommended. Where quilting thread may be used for added strength in hand piecing, this will not usually be necessary when sewing by machine. The stitch gauge is set to give about 12 stitches per inch (5 per cm).

Alignment of pieces to be sewn together and adequate pinning are as important here as with hand piecing. Pins may be set through two pieces of fabric in positions that will not interfere with the stitching (see Fig. 3-33). If pins must be placed across the path of the stitching, these should be removed just before they go under the presser foot. The needle point is easily burred when it comes into sudden contact with a pin and may be rendered useless.

Most new machines, and many older ones, come equipped with a seam guide incised on the plate beneath the presser foot. This will be marked with graded measurements about ⅛ in. (3 mm) apart.

The ¼-in. (6-mm) marking is used to gauge the seam allowance in machine piecing. With some machines, the edge of the presser foot may be used to determine the ¼-in. (6-mm) seam. If a gauge is not built in, one can be quickly improvised by taping a strip of paper with ⅛-in. (3-mm) intervals marked on it to the plate beneath the presser foot, ¼ in. (6 mm) to the right of the needle.

Sew each seam beginning at the edge of the fabric and proceeding through the opposite edge, as in Figs. 3-33 and 3-35. It is not necessary to backtack (guide the stitch forward and then backward at the beginning and end of a seam) as long as joined units are handled carefully throughout the piecing process. Care should be taken in guiding the fabric smoothly under the presser foot and in maintaining a consistent ¼-in. (6-mm) seam allowance. Sew each group of identical units at one sitting, continuing the same line of stitching through each unit without cutting the thread. This saves both time and thread (Fig. 3-33).

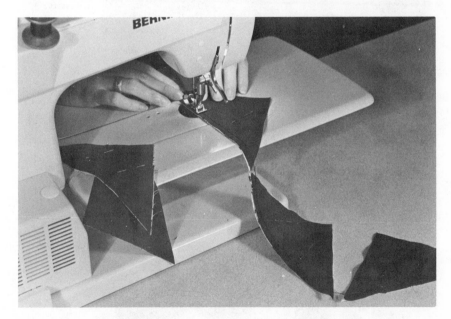

Figure 3-33   *Machine piecing.* Sets of identical units are sewn in one sitting, then pressed.

In machine piecing, each seamed unit must be pressed before it is sewn to other units. Press as with hand piecing, light under dark whenever possible. When joining cross-seams, pin pressed units together, carefully aligning seams and/or points so that they will meet accurately (Fig. 3-34). Continue to sew units together with a carefully guided ¼-in. (6-mm) seam allowance.

Figure 3-34 *Aligning seams.* Where four or more pieces join at a point, check to be sure seams correspond and pin accordingly.

Figure 3-35 Machine stitch from raw edge to raw edge; backtacking is not necessary.

Figure 3-36 *Finished block.*

The greatest portion of quilts made in this country since 1750 have been pieced. The nature of pieced construction is such that the process has lent itself to the use of scraps and pieces of used clothing as well as inexpensive fabric from the bolt. It has, in general, been popular because of the economy and thrift that it encourages. There also seems to be some magic in the notion that one can take an array of small fabric pieces and join them to form a large piece of designed fabric that up to that point did not exist. This long tradition of piecing quilts continues unabated into the late twentieth century, and although the motivation for making them has certainly changed in two hundred years, the fascination with the design possibilities of pieced work has not.

The author's quilt, "Elaborated Tangram" (Fig. 3-37 and Plates 1a and 1b), is a visually complex design that is based on the repetition of sixteen blocks, each identical in structure. Figure 3-38 shows a line drawing of one of the blocks, and the adjacent diagram shows how those blocks are arranged to imply a random "disorder" that is, in fact, strictly calculated. The basic geometric units of the ancient Chinese tangram puzzle are here multiplied within a 21-in. (53.5-cm) square. The actual straight seams between the blocks are in some places difficult to determine. Within the blocks, much of the piecing involved straight seams, although several seams in each were wide angles, sewn outward from the inner joint of the angle. All of the piecing in this quilt was done by hand, as was the quilting.

The initial design for "Elaborated Tangram" was worked out in pencil on graph paper. Colors were chosen from fabrics at hand, and the color distributions were worked out as the sewing progressed.

"Razzle Dazzle Quilt" (Plate 2 and Fig. 3-39) is another hand-pieced, repeated block design that, in the regularity of placement of each of the blocks, is more closely tied to a traditional arrangement. As is the nature of pieced blocks set together without lattice, several over-all designs seem to be apparent simultaneously as one's attention is focused on the quilt. The varitoned blue squares in each block are set into right angles formed by the joining of elongated parallelograms. The size and placement of the middle border parallelograms was carefully calculated to move naturally around the clipped bottom corners and to carry out the angles formed by the corners of the blocks at the white inner border (see Fig. 6-8). The lengths of border were attached to the quilt by machine.

Figure 3-37 *Elaborated Tangram*, by the author, 1976. Hand-pieced and hand-quilted cotton. 94″ x 94″. Photo by Bruce MacFarland.

"Tossed Salad Quilt" (Plates 3a and 3b) was designed to be entirely machine pieced. The "sawtooth" theme common in many traditional quilts is here emphasized by the free-hanging triangles at the bottom of the quilt. Strips of sawteeth of various sizes are arranged over the surface to give an abstract quality to the design. Attention is focused on the "central medallion" area surrounded by the visually rotating "Roman Stripe" border. The colors are those of a fresh summer salad.

44

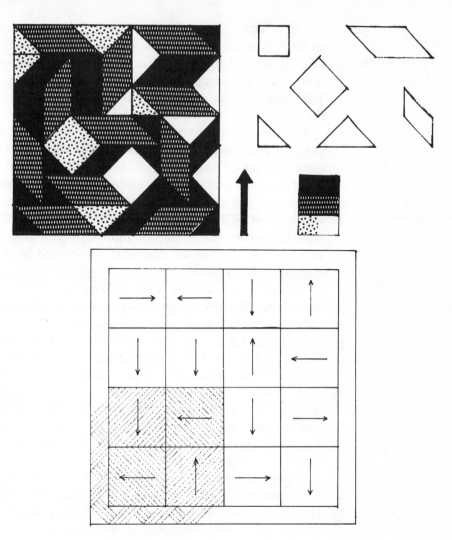

Figure 3-38   Construction diagram for *Elaborated Tangram.*

Figure 3-39   Detail, *Razzle Dazzle,* by the author.

Like "Tossed Salad," a small wall quilt by Jane Burke displays an interest in the traditional sawtooth motif. Here four repeat blocks (each is actually a small four-patch within a nine-patch within a four-patch) are grouped to form a strong, symmetrical composition. The warm, muted vegetable-dyed wools contrast effectively with the crispness of the sawteeth in the design (Plate 4).

The limited size of such small "wall" or "crib" quilts offers the quiltmaker a convenient format within which to experiment with pieced design. "Roman Stripe Composition Quilt" by the author is such a small-scale study in piecework. Shape, color, and light/dark contrasts break up the center of the two-dimensional surface, which is contained by the radiating striped border. The shaped form of the quilt intensifies the feeling of motion in the graded border (Plates 5a and 5b). The top of this quilt was pieced by machine, and the quilting done by hand.

A cool color scheme first interpreted in "Tossed Salad" and revised in "Roman Stripe Composition" is expanded in "Necker's Cube Quilt" (Plate 6) with the final elimination of the roses and the highlighting of the whites and blacks. This hand-pieced pattern is built on the conventional repeat of one block (see Fig. 3-32), which in this instance is a cube-within-a-cube illusion. Four of these blocks are grouped together to form larger repeat units (see Fig. 3-11), of which there are nine. The additional illusion of transparency within the design is intended to heighten the spatial attitude of the surface, and the indented outer edge likewise draws surrounding space into the quilt.

Nancy Halpern's "Round the Twist" (Plates 7a and 7b) is built on a nine-patch modification of the block illustrated in Fig. 3-4f. The subtle blending of the colors of clay, wood, and spring dew suggests the tonal harmony of the woodlands; and this harmony and unity is further emphasized by the interweaving of the design elements. This woven lattice is a familiar, two-dimensional, decorative device and can be found in Persian miniature painting as well as in the surface design of other cultures. In this hand-pieced and hand-quilted surface, it is represented with great sensitivity and superb craftsmanship.

A feeling of electricity charges the surface of Beth and Jeffrey Gutcheon's "Wicked Lily," a pieced design in which abstracted flower forms converge at the center in a staccatolike interplay of light and dark triangles. This intense activity enhances the kaleidoscopic quality of the image. The measured progression from the lightest ground at the center of the top to the darkest colors at the outer ring unifies all elements of the surface and works to pull the eye into the explosion of color and shape at the center.

The sensitive control with which the design elements are handled contrasts markedly with the spirit of abandon portrayed in the image itself (Plate 8).

The graphic intensity of Ethel Klane's "Checquered Diamonds" (Plate 9) reveals a strong appreciation of the communicative power of color. The dominant red figures are held to the subtle black-and-white stripe ground by accents of blue and green that serve also to suggest that several different visual planes are interacting here. Two blocks, each an arrangement of triangles and parallelograms and each only slightly different than the other, are ordered four-by-four within the larger format. Note that smaller, incomplete squares are formed at the center of each block, and these cleverly echo the shape of the blocks and of the quilt as a whole.

4 Appliqué

It is quite probable that the art of appliqué had its beginnings with the first use of a small fabric patch to repair a worn or damaged garment. The utilitarian application of "patches" to extend the life of clothing and furnishings must have led very quickly to the realization that such "appliqué" could have decorative uses as well.

As a quilt form, appliqué reached its American zenith during the nineteenth century, when it was used widely in creating the elegant "best" quilts of the period. These quilts, often made as wedding gifts or as commemorative pieces, were designed to spotlight the maker's way with elaborate floral motifs as well as her needlework skill. The inclination to use flowers and foliage as primary design elements of the appliqué surface reflected the quiltmaker's dependence on the natural world for inspiration.

This looking to nature can serve the contemporary quiltmaker as well, for where appliqué is concerned, all organic and free-forms are suitable material for reinterpretation on the appliqué quilt surface. Whether the image reflects a representational approach to the design problem or a nonfigurative, abstract conception of appliqué form and shape, the technique presents to the quiltmaker a pathway of unlimited creative potential.

DESIGN

Appliqué design can be divided into two categories. The first includes those designs that, as whole units, are clearly symmetrical in arrangement. The many hundreds of "rose" pattern variations of the nineteenth century are typical examples; as block designs, these are usually laid out against imaginary "axes" that divide the block into symmetrical parts (Fig. 4-1). The individual elements of the block design are likely to be identical shapes developed by folding pieces of paper and cutting out the figure.

The second category includes all of those designs and images that are freely drawn and cut from fabric and as freely arranged over the quilt surface. In the traditional quilt, this very often involved figurative or narrative images or scenarios designed in block form and set together with lattice strips or—less frequently—large, over-all compositions, less formal yet more personally expressive by nature. Just as the painter might manipulate form and space on canvas, so to could the patchworker, using appliqué, create fabric compositions. Indeed, this form as a folk art genre of the nineteenth and early twentieth centuries reveals a range of artistic accomplishment reflecting attitudes and sensibilities both naive and sophisticated. For the contemporary quiltmaker, use of this form can lead to equally creative experiences.

SYMMETRICAL APPLIQUÉ DESIGN

The simple, folded paper snowflake that most of us would recall having made at one time or another as children reflects the basic pattern-making technique for symmetrical appliqué design. As a means of drafting the pattern for appliqué, it is quick and simple and can be created in endless variety. The Hawaiian-style appliqué quilt is based, on a large scale, on this method of pattern preparation.

Lightweight brown wrapping paper is a durable material for making the patterns and is easily manipulated while cutting. For most designs of this type, the paper is folded to form either a square or a triangle, the folds determining the number of axes within the design. The size of the pattern is a matter of choice; but in exploring the technique, a suitable size for a sampler block would be from 12 to 18 in. (30.5 to 46 cm).

For a square pattern, simply fold the sheet in half, side to side, and then in half again, as in Fig. 4-1. It is helpful to run the edge of one's ruler along each fold as it is made, thus assuring a firm, crisp edge. This will, in turn, assure you that your design will be uniformly proportioned. The sheet, thus folded, will be one-quarter of its original size. The folds indicate the axes of the pattern, and it is along these that the design is drawn, producing a four-pointed image.

For a triangular pattern, fold the sheet in half, corner to corner, and twice more, always corner to corner (see Fig. 4-2). The resulting triangle will be one-eighth the original size of the sheet. Care must be taken that the corners match in folding and that the creases be sharp and firm. Once again, the folds indicate the axes of the design, producing here an eight-pointed image.

The triangular pattern was used to create the design shown in Fig. 4-3, which is a naturalistic study of a German Ivy leaf. The design takes on a character of its own, however, when the pattern is unfolded and becomes more distinctly abstract in form. The longest fold of the triangle becomes the main axis in this case, and the shorter fold is not used as an element of the pattern other than that it provides a bridge between each of the four "leaves."

Figure 4-1 *Symmetrical appliqué.*
Square pattern.

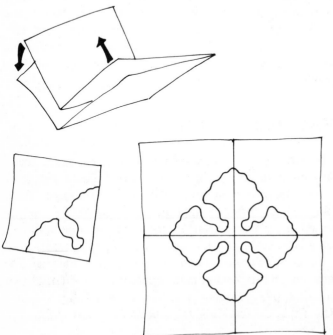

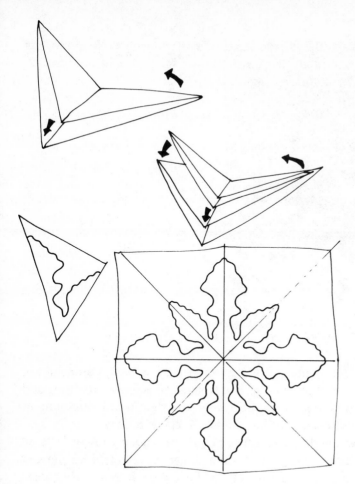

Figure 4-2 *Symmetrical appliqué.*
Diagonal pattern.

Figure 4-3 Diagram of *German Ivy*
diagonal fold pattern.

FREE-FORM APPLIQUÉ DESIGN

With the folded paper pattern method for appliqué, you need not be particularly accomplished as a draftsman to achieve satisfying and interesting results. Slight variations in the depth and direction of curves and contours can produce widely varying designs.

On the other hand, free-form appliqué, inasmuch as it reflects an artistic and original approach to the design problem, does depend in great measure on your ability to draw well and to "compose" a two-dimensional space, balancing all elements of the design so that they relate and form an integral "whole." Whereas the folded axial designs will by their nature achieve a physical and visual balance, free-form, nonrepeating images must depend on the careful manipulation of size, shape, and of spatial tension.

Although I hope that you will feel confident enough in your drawing abilities to begin to explore free-form design for appliqué, I understand that for some this may seem beyond reach in this initial exploration of the quilt as a creative medium. Suitable subject matter for appliqué can, however, be found in abundance in printed form, and just about any photograph or line drawing can be translated as appliqué.

To enlarge to the desired size any printed image or any original drawing you may have done, first trace all of the shape outlines, as well as the outer boundaries of the picture or sketch, on tracing paper. You will now have a simplified line drawing of the original image. Superimpose, with ruler and pencil, a square grid on the drawing, ruling the parallel lines from ¼ in. (6 mm) to 2 in. (5 cm) or 3 in. (7.5 cm) apart, depending on the size of the original you are working with. A ¼-in. (6-mm) or ½-in. (1.3-cm) grid will be necessary for very small pictures or drawings; a 1-in. (2.5-cm), 2-in. (5-cm), or 3-in. (7.5-cm) grid may be necessary when working from larger images. Once the grid has been marked out, determine how large you wish the final appliqué composition to be. On a large sheet of paper (brown wrapping paper is fine for this, too) rule out the enlargement of your grid. If, for example, you started with a 4 in. by 5 in. (10 cm by 12.5 cm) drawing over which you superimposed a grid of ½-in. (1.3-cm) squares and you wish the final size to be 24 in. by 30 in. (61 cm by 76 cm), you must draw the enlargement as a grid of 3-in. (7.5-cm) squares. Once this is done, carefully mark your shapes on the new grid, drawing into each square the corresponding lines and shapes from the original.

If you wish to enlarge only a small portion or a single shape from an original, you may follow the same procedure, applying the grid, however, only to the section you wish to enlarge.

When creating your own original designs for appliqué, it is a good idea to do the original drawing on graph paper. This eliminates the need to do a grid superimposition as a second step; you can simply draw an enlarged grid scaled to your graph paper drawing and complete the full-size pattern. In preparing the wall quilt, "Florescent Rag," I first made a sketch (Fig. 4-5a) on graph paper,

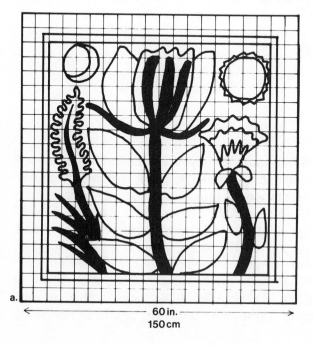

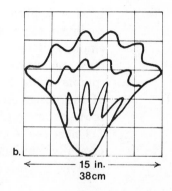

Figure 4-5 a. Preliminary sketch for *Florescent Rag.* b. Enlargement of coxcomb.

a.

← 60 in. →
150 cm

b.

← 15 in. →
38 cm

determining at the outset that each square would equal 3 in. in enlarged form. This provided a measurement of 48 in. (122 cm) for the central appliqué area, with an additional 6-in. (15-cm) border all around, for a total, over-all quilt size of 60 in. (150 cm). I proceeded to enlarge each figure in the composition singly, preferring to approximate the size and shape of each element, and thus allowing myself the freedom to alter contours and relative proportions within the confines of the enlarged grid of 3-in. (7.5-cm) squares. For example, having observed that the sun shape in the upper right occupied an area of sixteen squares in the original drawing, I ruled a 12 in. by 12 in. (30.5 cm by 30.5 cm) square on brown wrapping paper and drew the sun and its corona freehand within that square area.

Should you feel that you risk sacrificing a sense of spontaneity in your design by preparing the patterns with enlarged grids, you can easily draw your images full-size directly on paper, creating the pattern for each shape singly, or composing the full-size quilt design as a whole unit. In this instance it may be necessary, depending on the desired size, to tape large sheets of paper together to form the full surface.

Likewise, a sense of spontaneity will be generated by drawing directly on your fabric and then cutting the shapes or by cutting the forms right out of the fabric, "drawing" so to speak with scissors. This can be successful providing that careful visual consideration is given to relative proportions and to the refinement of line and form. Drawing directly on fabric, however, demands that every mark be well conceived and deliberate; only limited corrections and alterations can be made.

PREPARING TO SEW

In that appliqué offers a more flexible and unrestricted approach to linear expression than does pieced work, it demands a greater amount of care and attention in preparation. Sewing construction must be strong; all edges must be smooth and free of "pokes" (points along the edge at which unraveling occurs); and all pieces of the design must lie flat on the fabric ground, with no wrinkles sewn permanently into either the appliqué or the ground surfaces.

Once the pattern has been drafted onto paper, each shape is carefully cut out along the penciled lines, using utility scissors reserved for this purpose. These paper templates should be numbered or labeled to correspond to their counterparts in the original drawing. Templates for shapes that will be used a number of times as part of a repeat block design or an allover pattern should be cut with a razor knife from illustration board, as for pieced templates.

All fabric should be preshrunk and freshly pressed. When working with paper patterns, pin the pattern in place on the right side of the fabric, positioning it so that as much of the contour of the shape as possible is on the bias or near-bias of the fabric. For example, with either type of folded paper pattern described earlier in this chapter, place the major axes on the bias of the fabric. Not only does this save fabric; it also helps to assure a smooth edge when the seam allowance is basted under. Allow at least ¼ in. (6 mm) of fabric between edges of the template and any raw edges or selvages of the material. Once the paper template is pinned in place, carefully mark around its edge with a well-sharpened pencil, bearing down more heavily when the fabric is a dark or busy print (Fig. 4-6).

Figure 4-6   *Marking appliqué.* Marking is done on *right* side of fabric.

With cardboard templates, simply hold the pattern piece in place on the right side of the fabric and mark with pencil. It is important that the line be clear and precise, as this line indicates the outer finished dimensions of your piece and will be an important guide in clipping the seam allowance. Tailor's chalk or dressmaker's pencil will again be unsuitable for this marking, as the resulting line will not conform to the exact shape of the pattern and will likely rub away before the basting is complete.

Cut all fabric pieces ¼ in. (6 mm) larger than the finished size of the shape as you marked it on the fabric. When cutting into narrow spaces between elements of your design as in Fig. 4-7, where there may be less or little more than a ½-in. (1.3 cm) space to provide seam allowances, cut straight down into the "valley" up to but not through the pencil line.

When the fabric piece has been cut out, clip all curved edges to facilitate folding under the seam allowance. Scissors should be well sharpened so that the points of the blades can be used here. Clip into the seam allowance, always perpendicular to the penciled line, taking care to clip just up to, but not through, the line. Space clips at wider intervals on curves that are very gradual or almost straight and closer together where curves are more highly pronounced, as in Fig. 4-8. Do not clip outer points; these will be folded when basting is done.

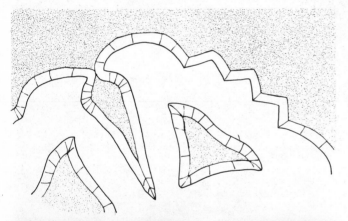

Figure 4-7 Clipping diagram for appliqué seams.

Figure 4-8 *Clipping seam allowance.*

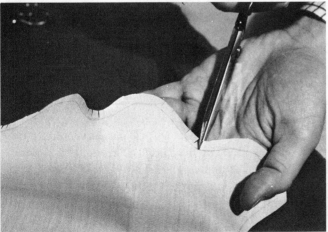

Although basting may at first seem a lengthy and tedious process, in the long run it saves time in appliqué by eliminating the need to do two things at once; that is, folding under the seam allowance and appliquéing simultaneously. It assures that your final appliqué piece will conform to the contours you planned for in drafting the design.

Use a number 8 sharp and a basting or other thread, preferably in a color that will contrast with the appliqué fabric. This will allow for quick removal of all basting once the sewing is complete. Hold the fabric piece right side up, and fold the allowance away from you, using the pencil line as your fold guide. As this is done, take a series of small basting stitches (in the same fashion as the running stitch is worked in piecing), being careful that all clipped sections of the seam are secured. Proceed along the edge of the piece, folding carefully on the line, and simply backstitch once when ending a length of thread. Figure 4-9 shows a properly basted appliqué edge.

Figure 4-9   *Basting seam allowance.*

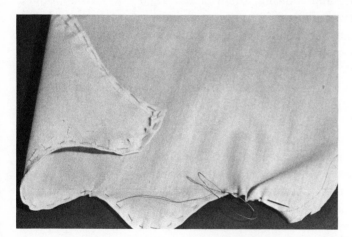

Once the seams have been basted, it remains to baste the pieces in place on the ground or foundation fabric. Press this larger piece (but do not press the appliqué), and lay it flat on a smooth surface. It may be helpful, especially with the symmetrical folded paper patterns, to lightly rule guidelines on the ground fabric from corner to corner and middle side to middle side, so that the figure can be centered on the ground square. Baste the appliqué piece(s) in place, using a large stitch and following the rough contour of the shape (Fig. 4-10). Pin basting is unsuitable in appliqué, as the pins inevitably dislodge in handling and can easily cause painful interruptions as the appliqué proceeds.

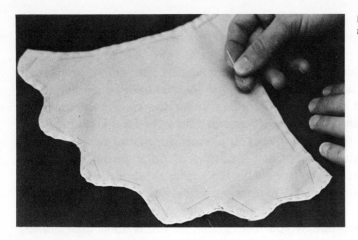

Figure 4-10 *Basting prepared piece to foundation.*

HAND APPLIQUÉ

As with piecing and quilting, there is no "right" way to appliqué; each person sews a little differently, and different methods may still produce very similar results. Two of those methods will be shown here. Whichever technique you choose to use in appliqué, keep in mind that the over-all neatness of the piece (smooth edges with no pokes and no fraying) and the size and uniformity of the stitches will greatly influence the "look" of your design.

I have preferred the use of a "blind" stitch or invisible stitch in appliqué; though it seems to demand a bit more skill and concentration in manipulating needle and fabric and does demand more practice to master, it results in workmanship that is at once more refined and more durable. Slight irregularities in the size and placement of stitches will not be apparent, and since the thread is not exposed to direct wear and abrasion, the life of the piece is prolonged.

Use a number 8 sharp for appliqué; thread color should match the appliqué fabric, and quilting thread is desirable. To begin, draw the needle through to the top from the back of the ground fabric, thus securing the knot on the wrong side of the work. Proceed to appliqué by guiding the point of the needle into the fold at the basted edge of the appliqué piece; then into the ground, catching two or three threads; then back into the fold and so on until the needle is "loaded" with stitches, as in Figs. 4-11 and 4-12. At this point, draw the needle up from the ground fabric and thus away from the work; then begin again by going into the fold of the appliqué. Note that the needle is drawn through completely only when it is "loaded" with stitches. Care must be taken so that the needle does not come through the top surface of the appliqué fabric but is guided only into the fold where the seam is turned under. (That the needle will show through once in a while is unavoidable, and so the color of the thread will help to disguise the intrusion.) Remember that the needle is drawn up from the right side of the work when taking stitches, and not through to the back.

It may be helpful to hold the fabric in such a way that you can clearly see the edge of the fold and the slight "S-curve" that the thread will make as it moves from appliqué to ground. When you reach any point where unraveling has occurred or in a "valley" where clipping has left little or no seam allowance, use a tight series of overcast stitches to reinforce the appliqué. Here again, using thread to match the appliqué will help to disguise the stitching.

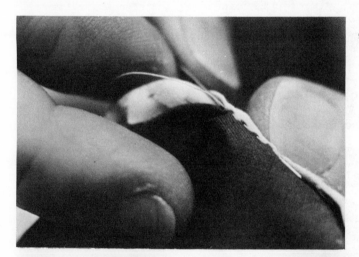

Figure 4-11 *Blindstitch.* Needle is guided alternately into fold and ground.

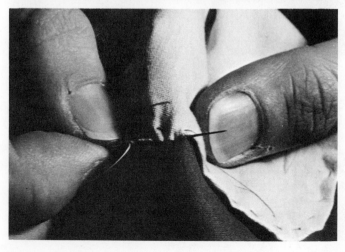

Figure 4-12 *Blindstitch.* Needle is loaded with stitches, then drawn up from ground.

The overcast stitch may be used as well to finish the entire appliqué edge. The thread is drawn up from the back of the ground fabric, but the needle is guided up through the surface of the appliqué just at the folded edge. The needle is then guided back into the ground ¹⁄₁₆ to ⅛ in. (1.5 mm to 3 mm) away from the point where it came up through the appliqué. Care should be taken that the stitch be perpendicular to the folded edge. The needle is then guided back up through the appliqué fabric just a bit ahead of the last stitch (Figs. 4-13, 4-14, and 4-15). This distance between stitches varies from quiltmaker to quiltmaker but should be kept uniform throughout the work.

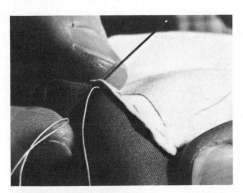

Figure 4-13 *Overcast stitch.* Needle is guided up through top surface at edge of appliqué piece.

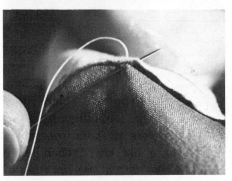

Figure 4-14 *Overcast stitch.* Needle enters ground fabric perpendicular to point from which thread has exited.

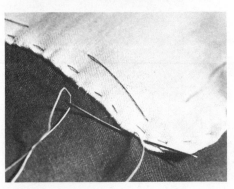

Figure 4-15 *Overcast stitch.* Stitches are about 1/8 in. (3 mm) apart.

To end a thread, pull up any slack, being careful not to gather the fabric and thus pucker the edge. Hide a double knot under the appliqué piece or on the back side of the work.

When all sewing is completed, remove the basting and press the entire piece. If quilting is to follow, it is advisable after pressing to cut away the ground fabric behind each appliqué piece to within ¼ in. (6 mm) of the stitched edge (see Fig. 4-16). This provides an even, one-thickness layer for quilting. It also eliminates the possibility that a dark-colored fabric ground will show through an appliqué that is not opaque, thus discoloring it.

Figure 4-16 Ground fabric is removed from behind appliqué, up to within 1/4 in. (6 mm) of stitching line.

MACHINE APPLIQUÉ

For machine appliqué, follow all of the steps in preparation up to and including the basting of the appliqué fabric to the ground. Particular care should be taken that the seam allowance be evenly folded under with no pokes and no unraveling visible.

Choose either a matching thread or, for effect, a contrasting color. For a simple straight stitch, set the machine to sew 8 to 12 stitches per inch (about 4 per cm), depending on the degree of delineation you wish to have in your topstitching. Carefully sew along the folded edge of the appliqué. When turning corners of acute curves, lift the presser foot and adjust the fabric to maintain a consistent distance between the stitching and the actual edge of the appliqué (see detail, Fig. 5-26). Do not backstitch when beginning or ending; thread ends should be pulled through to the back of the piece with a needle and knotted or "woven" into the stitching (Fig. 4-17).

Decorative machine stitches may also be used for appliqué. These should be chosen carefully so that they complement the overall "sense" of the appliqué surface.

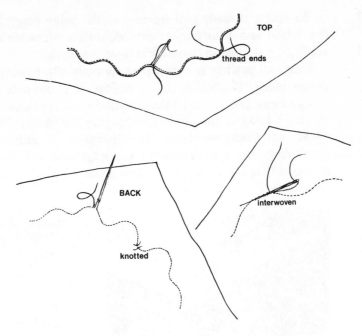

Figure 4-17   Knotting off thread ends for machine stitching.

SOME CONTEMPORARY APPLIQUÉ QUILTS

As one takes a backward glance at the development of traditional patchwork design, one senses a fundamental difference in pieced work and appliqué that goes beyond the obvious contrast of straight, angular shapes with curvilinear, free-flowing forms. Pieced design develops out of the realm of abstract thought and idea; it is non-representational for the most part. Its forms may be intended to function as symbols and may call to mind natural phenomena (although this was more often the result of associations suggested by the pattern titles rather than the designs themselves). The power of the pieced image is primarily evocative; the contrasts of light and dark shapes, of angle and line, and especially of color arouse emotional responses in the viewer that are not, or need not be, dependent on association with aspects of the physical world.

Appliqué design, on the other hand, has explored the relationships of man and nature in a more narrative way. Much appliqué imagery was inspired by observation of the plant and animal life with which the quiltmaker was familiar. These representations in fabric served not only to decorate the two-dimensional surface of the quilt but also to document and record the interaction of the quiltmaker with the world around her. Certainly the imagery in the appliqué quilt might be highly stylized, or indeed abstract. Nevertheless, the unrestricted movement of line and of each shape in general would have necessitated drawing on personal visual experiences and responses to nature, however subconscious these might have been.

The tradition is ongoing. "Janie's Alphabet" (Fig. 4-18), for example, assembles an unlikely menagerie of our beastly brethren in a surface whose simplified graphic forms appeal to child and adult alike. The animal caricatures in tie silks, satin, velvet, and uncut corduroy recall the use of such fabrics in the late nineteenth century "crazy" throw, often embellished—as here—with decorative embroidery. Indeed, just as many of the antique examples were without actual quilting, so has Jane Burke joined top and backing with decorative French knots rather than with quilting. Buttons, beads, bells and an antique silver needle case embellish the surface, adding sparkle and necessary detail to the figures (see Fig. 6-21 for close-up).

The stylizations populating "Alphabet" are seen again parading across the hand-appliquéd poplin hanging shown in Plate 11.

"Florescent Rag" (Plate 10) by the author was appliquéd entirely by hand, using the blind stitch described in this chapter. After the

Figure 4-18 *Janie's Alphabet*, by Jane Burke, 1975. Hand piecing and appliqué. Satin, silk, velvet, and other fabrics, 96" x 96".

sewing was completed, all ground fabric behind the appliquéd pieces was removed to assure an even, single-thickness surface for quilting. Designed as a wall quilt, the pictorial arrangement emphasizes the stagelike setting in which the exaggerated flower forms dance in a nocturnal ballet witnessed by sun, moon, and stars. The exotic plume, the poppy, and the two coxcombs were inspired by similar floral stylizations in traditional appliqué quilts, hooked rugs, and embroideries.

In "Brill" (Plate 12), Nancy Crow has combined both piecing and reverse appliqué in constructing a surface where movement is suggested by the dramatic use of color gradations and the clockwise rotation of the large red triangles and semicircles. (Reverse appliqué, as contrasted with direct appliqué, is a technique by which one cuts through a top layer of fabric to expose another fabric color beneath. Edges of the top layer are turned under and sewn onto the second layer.) The central area, surrounded by the haphazard sawtooth border, displays dark-to-light value gradations of blue moving to the left and of blue-green moving to the right. The whole effect is one of sharp brilliance and repeated motion.

5 Quilting

The word *quilting* refers to the series of small stitches sewn through the layers of the quilt to secure them as one. It serves several additional functions. It gives increased strength to the quilt—particularly to one that is hand-pieced or appliquéd—by permanently fixing the patchwork top to a backing, thus preventing any shifting or stretching of the top. It anchors the batting material between the two fabric layers, minimizing the chance that the batting will tear and bunch up during use and washing. Perhaps most importantly, quilting can give to a quilt surface the characteristically subtle, over-all texture as well as additional design interest when thoughtful consideration is given to its relationship to the linear and rhythmic elements of the patchwork design. Indeed, in the whole-cloth quilt where there is no patchwork, the quilting is usually the sole basis for creating surface design.

The decorative possibilities of quilting were well recognized by eighteenth and nineteenth century needleworkers, and it is often the closely quilted masterpieces of those eras that we admire today. Few modern quilters, however, would venture to quilt surfaces in parallel lines ¼ in. (6 mm) or ⅛ in. (3 mm) apart; and to be sure, many quilts from the past display only a minimum of quilting. However, such minimums, even today, should not be determined solely by a functional need to hold the layers together but also by a desire to enhance the beauty of the quilt surface.

Hand quilting is a slow, inch-by-inch process that cannot be hurried. With practice, one is able to work up to a fairly steady speed and to develop a rhythmic pace, much in the way that a hand weaver develops and works with a rhythm at the loom, or a hand spinner at the wheel. The quilter gradually becomes "one" with the process, enjoying the continuous repetition of motion as the needle is guided into and drawn through the fabric layers. It is during the quilting process that the quiltmaker gets to know at very close range every detail of a quilt's surface.

DESIGN

There are no set rules for determining appropriate quilting designs for a given project. You are free to be as imaginative as you like. Whether you choose to use pencil and ruler to work out a geometric solution or prefer to draw freehand designs (quilting is, after all, a form of drawing, as it deals primarily with line), the possibilities are limitless.

One of the best ways to become acquainted with the uses and application of quilting designs is to study old quilts from museum textile collections. It is here that one often finds a high degree of artistry and originality in the handling of quilting motifs. An understanding of how quilters of past generations integrated the quilting pattern with the patchwork design will facilitate the process of choosing and drafting a pattern for a contemporary adaptation or an original quilt design.

Figure 5-1 shows several "filler" patterns that, though fairly commonplace, serve to hold the layers together and give surface texture to the quilt. These are allover patterns that help to unify the surface without necessarily being integrated with the pieced or appliqué design. Simple filler patterns can be especially helpful in quilting an otherwise complex and busy pieced or appliqué surface and often work well in contrast to the more elaborate, curvilinear designs in wide, solid-color borders or in open color-field areas (see detail of "Bedloe's Island Pavement Quilt," Plate 15b).

Of the traditional approaches to quilting design, outline quilting is the most commonplace solution. The quilting follows the shape of

Figure 5-1 *Traditional filler quilting designs.*

each piece in the pattern, usually about ⅛ in (3 mm) or ¼ in. (6 mm) from the seam line within each shape. Although it adequately serves to hold the layers together and secure the batting, and does emphasize the pieces in the top design, as a whole it tends to lack interest and usually shows little imagination on the part of the quilter. In order to follow the shape of every piece in the quilt top, the quilter working at a frame must often sew in awkward or uncomfortable positions, and the quilter working with a hoop must constantly turn and reposition the work.

Figure 5-2   *Quilting diagrams for traditional blocks.*

Outline quilting of appliqué patterns, on the other hand, often gives added fluidity and grace to the design. Quilting on the background fabric follows the shapes of the appliqué pieces about ¼ in. (6 mm) from the stitched edge (hence the term *echo quilting*). In Hawaiian-style appliqué quilts, outline quilting usually radiates out to the edge of the quilt in concentric lines beginning at the edge of the appliqué piece and spaced from about ½ in. (1.3 cm) to 1 in. (2.5 cm) apart (see Fig. 4-3).

An implied direction suggested by light and dark shapes within a pieced design will often lead to a geometric pattern that complements that design and adds interest to the quilt (both top and backing) as well. Figure 5-2 illustrates possible solutions to the drafting of quilting designs for a series of traditional pieced blocks. The quilting designs are based on the standard light-dark arrangements for those patterns. Just as the block patterns themselves will create secondary patterns when placed one to the next, so too will the quilting patterns for these blocks join to form all-over designs.

Freehand line drawing, particularly on solid fabric, can be an interesting and refreshing alternative to the more typical formality of traditional quilting designs. Elements of the physical environment (figures, faces, natural objects, and so on) as well as linear compositions of a nonrepresentational nature may be particularly adaptable to nontraditional pieced and/or appliqué surfaces (see Fig. 5-27).

MARKING

In most cases it is necessary to plan the quilting design, occasionally on paper, prior to its application to the quilt surface. The quilting lines are marked on the top to insure against uneven and haphazard sewing. This may be done in several ways.

The most widely used method, and the most direct, is to mark the quilting design in number two pencil or a colored chalk pencil directly on the fabric. In geometric quilt patterns, this is usually done by marking with a ruler block-by-block, uniformly measuring points along the outside of the blocks and/or within them to assure alignment of the over-all pattern (Fig. 5-3). Depending on personal preference, this marking may be done before the top is secured to batt and backing or after the basting of the layers is complete,

Figure 5-3 *Marking.* Quilting pattern being marked with ruler and pencil.

providing at all times that care is exercised to assure straight lines and uniform spacing. Uneven or irregular marking based on ruler measurement is due more often to inaccurate piecing than it is to the effect of the batting thickness on the marking. The quilter who wishes to mark a small section at a time as the quilting progresses may feel perfectly comfortable in doing so.

A well-sharpened pencil is used to do most marking. The pencil should be drawn lightly along the edge of the ruler, so as to leave a fine line that is just visible. The pencil markings are removed by washing the quilt once it is finished. Avoid making heavy markings

Figure 5-4 Detail, *Meadow Lily*, by the author.

that are difficult to remove. On some printed fabrics, particularly darker ones, it may be difficult to see the penciled line. In this case, an artist's white chalk or drawing pencil, well sharpened, should be used. Dressmaker's chalk pencils are not recommended as they are not easily sharpened and tend to rub off well before the quilting is completed.

When using paper or cardboard templates or stencils (Fig. 5-5) the pencil should likewise be drawn lightly along the edge of the pattern. The stencil for the twisted cable border used on the quilt in Fig. 5-6 was copied from a traditional source onto illustration board, and a narrow channel for pencil marking was cut with an Exacto knife.

Figure 5-5   *Marking with stencil.*

Figure 5-6   *Meadow Lily*, by the author, 1974. Hand pieced and appliqué, hand quilted cotton, 84″ x 84″.

Transferring nongeometric quilting designs to the fabric surface (especially in the case of whole-cloth quilts or plain blocks) may be done in several ways. Perforated quilting patterns for traditional designs are available commercially for this purpose. The pattern is pinned in place on the fabric surface, and a dusting of cinnamon (for light-colored fabrics) or cornstarch or French chalk (for darker fabrics) is rubbed through the perforations with a soft cloth or cotton ball. The pattern is then carefully removed, and the dusted impression is lightly penciled over. When this marking is completed, the dust is brushed or shaken off the surface, and the quilting may proceed (see Figs. 5-7 and 5-8)

Figure 5-7 *Marking with perforated pattern.* Cinnamon is rubbed through holes in tracing paper.

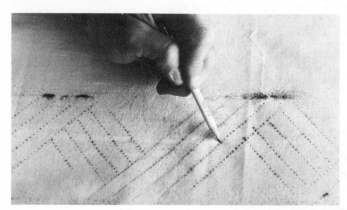

Figure 5-8 Pencil lines are marked lightly over dusted impression, then cinnamon is brushed off.

Perforated patterns of original designs are easily made on heavy-weight tracing paper. The drawing is first done in pencil directly on the tracing paper. The perforation of this line drawing is then done on an unthreaded sewing machine set for 6 stitches per in. (or about 3 per cm). The drawing is carefully guided under the presser foot as the opposite hand turns the wheel to raise and lower the needle.

The perforating may also be done with the use of a pushpin or small nail. Once the perforation is complete, the reverse side of the pattern is rubbed lightly with a fine sandpaper to fully open the holes. As the process of perforating the pattern by machine can be time-consuming, depending on the intricacy of the design, it is recommended only for patterns that will be used extensively in the quilt such as repeated designs for alternate plain blocks, borders, and the like.

Quilting designs may also be transferred to the quilt surface by means of a dressmaker's tracing wheel and tracing carbon. The line-drawing pattern is pinned in place on the fabric surface, and tracing carbon in an appropriate color (e.g., white or yellow on dark fabrics; yellow, red, or blue on lighter fabrics) is slipped under the paper pattern, carbon side against the fabric. The tracing wheel is then guided along the lines of the design (Fig. 5-9). The tracing wheel that produces a dotted line is preferred to that which makes a solid line.

Figure 5-9 *Marking with tracing wheel.* Dressmaker's carbon is placed right side to fabric, and wheel is guided over pattern.

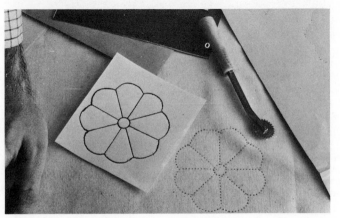

Figure 5-10 *Completed pattern.*

Sheets of semitransparent Mylar (available from architects' supply shops) make long-lasting and durable pattern sheets for use with the tracing wheel, which will not perforate this paper-thin plastic. The design is drawn on the Mylar, and the marking proceeds as with regular paper patterns. The author's quilt "Night Sky 1" (Fig. 5-11) was marked in this fashion. The two block designs (Fig. 5-12) were first drawn in pencil on 8-in. (20.5-cm) squares of the Mylar. The whole-cloth fabric surface (pieced along a center seam from two full widths of fabric) was then ruled with white pencil into a grid of fifty-six 8-in. (20.5-cm) squares, seven-by-eight. The patterns were, in turn, placed carefully on the fabric, held in place as the carbon was inserted, and marked with the tracing wheel (Fig. 5-13). Once the entire design had been transferred to the fabric, the three layers were basted together, and the quilting begun.

Figure 5-11 *Night Sky 1*, by the author, 1976. Hand-quilted polished cotton; polyester batting, 74″ x 90″. Photo by Bruce MacFarland.

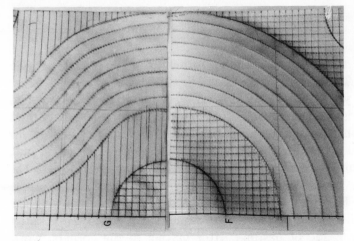

Figure 5-12 *Quilting patterns for "Night Sky 1."* Patterns were drawn on sheets of transparent Mylar.

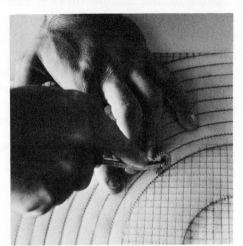

Figure 5-13 *Marking Mylar pattern with tracing wheel.*

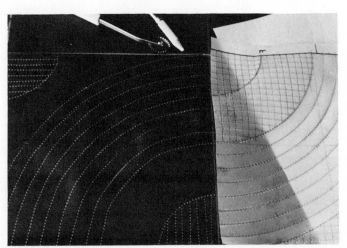

Figure 5-14 *Completed marking.*

The top and the backing should be freshly pressed in preparation for the basting. The backing (see Chap. 6) is laid seams up on a large, flat surface (your floor is the likeliest place to baste a large project). The batting is then placed carefully on the backing and smoothed out to eliminate wrinkles. Finally, the top is placed right side up on these two layers and any unevenness here is in turn eased out.

The basting is done by eye, following the diagram in Fig. 5-15. Begin at the center, working diagonally outward to each corner. Use a single thickness of thread, which may be cut rather long for this work. The thread is knotted to begin, and a backstitch is taken when ending a line of basting. After basting to the corners, work out from the center to the middle of each side. Next, following the general shape of the project, baste outward from the center in concentric units spaced from 8 in. (20.5 cm) to 10 in. (25.5 cm) apart. Basting stitches need be no smaller than 3 in. (7.5 cm) to 4 in. (10 cm). A final outline row of basting should enclose the very edge of the three layers to help prevent batting at the raw edge from separating.

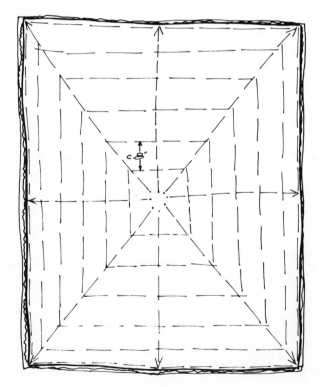

Figure 5-15   *Quilt-basting diagram.*

Great care should be taken in basting that the backing fabric not wrinkle while the sewing proceeds. It may be helpful to tape or tack the backing to the work surface before laying on the middle and top layers. As one hand guides the needle through the sandwich, the other should smooth out the layers and ease out any surface unevenness.

HAND QUILTING

I use a number 8 quilting needle, often called a "between," and recommend this for quilting. A between is a short, narrow needle with a fine eye easily capable of accommodating the standard ply quilting threads.

The thread used is a moderate weight (about a number 40) cotton thread usually available as "quilting" thread (see Fig. 2-1). It is manufactured with a glacé finish that helps to strengthen the thread and prevent knotting. There are no specific rules that govern choice of color in thread for quilting. In most cases, large areas of solid fabric are quilted in a matching thread; however, interesting effects may result when fabric is quilted in a contrasting color. It should be kept in mind, however, that any irregularities in size and spacing of stitches will be exaggerated if quilting has been done in a contrasting thread. On prints, particularly highly figured designs, the thread itself may not be readily apparent and should not be so if the stitches are small and uniform. In scrapbag or multichrome quilts, one color thread is generally used throughout, and this is chosen for its ability to blend inconspicuously into the grounds of the fabric. In general, *the quilting stitch itself should be less apparent than the indentation it forms in the surface of the quilt.*

The use of thimbles is necessary in quilting. For the right-handed quilter the thimbles are worn on the middle finger of the sewing (right) hand and on the index finger of the left hand, working beneath the quilt. For the left-handed quilter, the positioning is reversed—thimbles on the middle finger of the left hand and index finger of the right.

Quilting should be done with the three layers securely stretched taut in either a full-size frame or a large, round wooden quilting hoop, about 23 in. (58.5 cm) in diameter. The portability of the hoop makes its use more practical, as does the fact that it does not require a large amount of space in which to be permanently set up, as does the quilting frame. The hoop may be set in its own stand, or propped against the edge of a table or other similar support, thus leaving both hands free to quilt.

The basted quilt layers should be pulled taut in the hoop as the bolt is tightened. Care should be taken to pull the fabric layers evenly in all directions, so that there is no distortion of the shapes in the surface design. Such distortions usually become permanent once the area is quilted. The use of the hoop in this manner helps to eliminate the possibility of quilting wrinkles into the quilt, especially on the reverse side of the work. It also promotes the uniform "low-relief" surface texture characteristic of quilts by causing the fabric space between the lines of quilting to puff up once the hoop tension is released. This is especially important to keep in mind when using cotton batting, which does not have the natural heft and "spring" peculiar to synthetic batts.

When quilting outer borders and edges as well as outer corners of quilts, the round hoop may be used successfully by extending the surface area of the quilt with muslin strips, as in Fig. 5-16. The strips should be about 6 in. (15 cm) to 8 in. (20.5 cm) wide and can be any length you desire beyond a minimum of about 30 in. (76 cm). Fold over about 1 in. (2.5 cm) of the muslin along one long side, and baste through this edge into the edge of the quilt. Two muslin strips will be needed at the corners, and these will overlap as illustrated. The hoop may also be used for small projects (such as pillows, hangings, and so on) that are not in themselves large enough to be stretched evenly. Strips of muslin are basted along all sides of the project, thus allowing it to be accommodated in the hoop.

The thread length for quilting should not exceed 18 in. (46 cm), and a somewhat shorter length is preferable. Long threads knot easily and tend to wear out before the sewing is completed. Waxing the thread with a cake of beeswax will help to strengthen it.

Figure 5-16 Muslin strips are basted to edges of quilt so that work may be accommodated in hoop.

A small knot is made in one end, and the sewing is done with a single strand. To begin, secure the knot within the batting by directing the needle into the top and batting a short distance from the line on which the quilting is to be done; bring the needle up on the line, and tug lightly on the thread to pop the knot into the middle layer (Fig. 5-17).

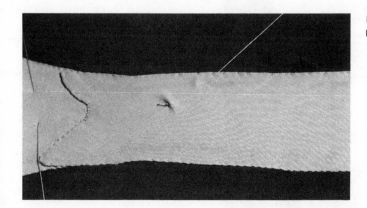

Figure 5-17 *Hand quilting.* Knot is popped into middle layer from top.

Hold the needle at about its mid-point with the thumb and index finger of the sewing hand. The needle should be held so that the eye is firmly set into one of the indentations in the textured side of the thimble (Fig. 5-18). The needle is guided into the quilt at a slight angle to the surface, directing the point of the needle through all three layers to the thimble below, against which it slides as it is directed back up again through the top (Fig. 5-19). I prefer to take one stitch at a time, pulling the thread through completely after each (Fig. 5-20). The regular repeat of these motions promotes the development of a steady quilting rhythm.

Figure 5-18 *Hand quilting.* Eye of needle is set into side of upper thimble. Needle is directed toward top edge of bottom thimble.

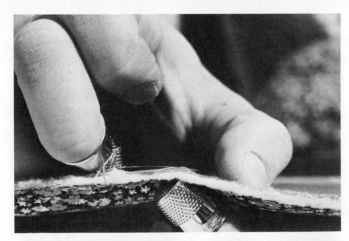

Figure 5-19 Thimble pushes needle off edge of bottom thimble.

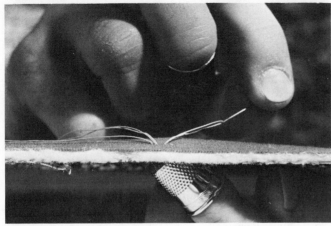

Figure 5-20 Stitches are taken one at a time.

The bottom hand is held palm-up so that the index finger with the thimble can be aimed at the needle entering from above. The edge of the lower thimble pushes up against the backing just below the quilting line so that a ridge is formed on the top side of the quilt (see Fig. 5-19). The needle is guided from above into this ridge (and against the edge of the lower thimble) and then pushed back up through the top with the side of the upper thimble (Fig. 5-21). The thumb of the quilting hand simultaneously presses down on the quilting line ahead of that point through which the needle and thread will emerge to begin the next stitch. This motion of the thumb helps to achieve small, uniform spaces between the stitches.

The thimble that is held beneath the quilt serves both to protect the finger and to help gauge even spacing and small stitches. The quilting needle touches the thimble, thus assuring that the thread will pass completely through to the back, and slides off the edge as it is directed back up through the top (Fig. 5-21). As long as the bottom thimble is held in the same position relative to the quilting line, a good degree of consistency in spacing will be maintained.

The size of the quilting stitch itself (that portion of the thread visible on the surface of the quilt) depends on the quilter's ability to set the tip of the needle back into the fabric at a point very close to where the thread has come up from the reverse side. At first, this will require a fairly deliberate and conscious effort; with practice, gauging the size of each stitch will become a relatively habitual reflex action integrated into the rhythmic process of quilting. Simply keep in mind that as soon as the needle touches the quilt surface on its way through the three layers, the size of the stitch has been determined. The more thread exposed in the quilting stitch, the greater are the chances that this thread will wear and break over a long period of time.

It is much more important for the over-all look of the quilt to work toward neatness and uniformity in the stitches and spacing than toward a set number of stitches per inch. Though this point is frequently mentioned as a qualification in judging workmanship in quilts, it is not entirely valid, especially if the judgment is based on comparisons to historical examples. Fabric weight and thickness of battings varied greatly a century ago, as they do today, and these are prime factors in determining how many stitches can be taken to the inch.

Figure 5-21 Top view showing ridge made by bottom thimble.

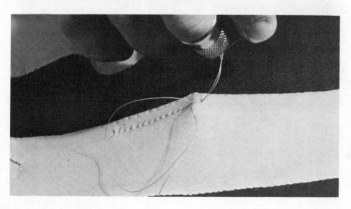

Figure 5-22 Needle is drawn up through top after each stitch.

To end a line of quilting, take a small backstitch through the top layer and batting, coming back up through the surface at the same point where the thread had initially emerged after the last stitch (Fig. 5-23). You will actually form a loop. Pull the thread taut, and pierce that stitch with the point of the needle, thus anchoring it in place (Fig. 5-24). Guide the needle in the batting a short distance from the stitch (about ¾ in., or 2 cm), draw it up through the top, and cut the thread at the surface (Fig. 5-25).

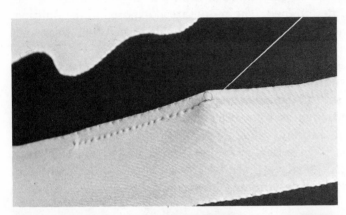

Figure 5-23 *Ending quilting.* Backstitch is taken and pulled tight.

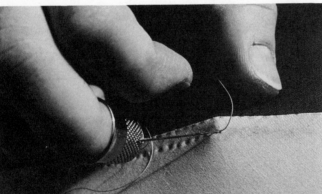

Figure 5-24 Needle pierces the backstitch and is then guided into batting.

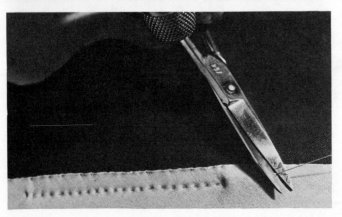

Figure 5-25 Thread is drawn up through top about one needle length from point where quilting ended; thread is cut at surface.

The key to enjoyment of the quilting process is the eventual development of a rhythm based on the continuous manipulation of the needle through the layers of the quilt. This comes only with practice and perseverance, both of which promise that the process, once mastered, need not be painstaking.

MACHINE QUILTING

You may prefer to quilt your work by machine. The two processes are obviously quite different in technique as well as in effect. The hand-stitched quilting line forms a soft, broken depression in the quilt sandwich. Machine quilting, on the other hand, results in a sharp, well-defined indentation. The visibility of tiny, regular hand stitches is reduced by the depression made in the quilt surface by the line of stitching. Machine stitches are much more evident, particularly when the thread does not match the fabric on which the quilting is done.

Neither process is necessarily better than the other, although from a practical viewpoint no one would dispute the fact that machine quilting is stronger. The two are different, and the choice of using one rather than the other must again be based on the intent of the quiltmaker and/or the aesthetic demands of the piece.

The three layers of the quilt should be thoroughly basted together to prevent any shifting while the sewing is done. A cotton-covered polyester thread may be used in the bobbin, and an all-cotton quilting thread on top. The bobbin thread should match the backing fabric, and the quilting thread should complement the fabrics in the top.

Set the machine to take from 12 to 14 stitches per inch (5 per cm). Begin by manually guiding the needle down into the layers; proceed without backtacking along the marked line. Thread ends should be drawn through to the back and woven over several stitches before being drawn into the batting and cut. (See explanation for ending machine appliqué and Fig. 4-17.)

If the piece being quilted is large, it may be necessary to roll up the layers under the arm of the machine to facilitate handling. Use your hands to smooth out the work being fed under the needle, taking care that wrinkles are not sewn in at points where stitched lines cross. In quilting curvilinear designs, it will be necessary to lift the presser foot occasionally to turn the work in order to move smoothly around corners and curves.

Figure 5-26 shows a detail of both machine appliqué and quilting, and a full view of the sampler is shown in Fig. 4-4.

Whether quilting by hand or by machine, it is probably best to quilt outward from the center of the piece, always moving away from completed areas. *Never quilt alternately in different areas of the piece separated by unquilted space*, unless the design of the quilt calls for these areas to remain unquilted.

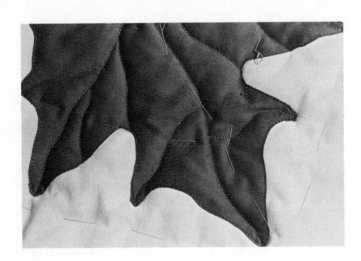

Figure 5-26   Detail, *Machine quilting and appliqué sampler.*

CONTEMPORARY QUILTING

Quiltmakers seem to have several things in common. They love fabric, or perhaps more specifically, they love to feel and to manipulate fabric. They appreciate the different appearances of fabric: the wrinkled or crisply pressed yardage, the very slight puckering along the handstitched seam, or the final gathering and puckering of the fabric surface as the quilting is done. They respond to the interplay of highlight and soft shadow across the quilted top; and this chiaroscuro, constantly changing as different light affects the surface, attracts the eye and invites the hand to touch.

Tactile appeal is only part of the reason why the whole-cloth quilt can be so effective. As I noted earlier, quilting is another form of drawing and as such offers unlimited opportunity for personal expression in fabric.

"Night Sky 1" by the author is an example of the use of quilting as the primary element in the design of the quilt surface. Inspired in part by those occasional stormy yet moonlit night skies, this

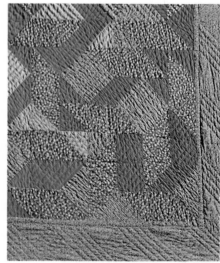

Plate 1a (above left)
Elaborated Tangram
Hand-pieced and hand-quilted
cotton, 94″ x 94″
(author, 1976)

Plate 1b (above right)
Detail, *Elaborated Tangram*

Plate 2 (right)
Razzle Dazzle. Hand- and
machine-pieced, hand-quilted
cotton, 84″ x 96″. Collection
of Joan Kaufmann-Wolfson

Plate 3a
Tossed Salad Quilt
Machine-pieced, hand-quilted
cotton, 90″ x 102″
(author, 1976)

Plate 3b (above)
Detail, *Tossed Salad Quilt*

Plate 4 (left)
Farmscape. Hand-pieced and
hand-quilted wool, 33" x 33"
(Jane Burke, 1976)

Plate 5a (above left)
Roman Stripe Composition Quilt
Machine-pieced, hand-quilted
cotton, 48'' x 48'' if square
(author, 1977). Collection of
Mr. and Mrs. Robert James III

Plate 5b (below left)
Detail,
Roman Stripe Composition Quilt

Plate 6 (below)
Necker's Cube Quilt
Hand-pieced, hand-quilted
cotton; polyester batting,
76'' x 76'' (author, 1977)

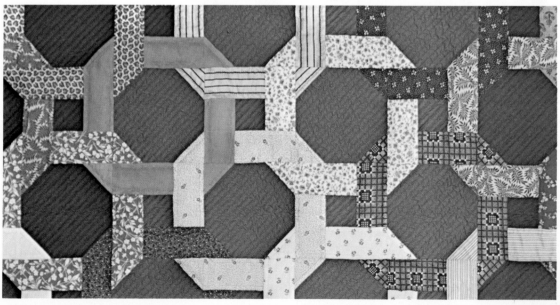

Plate 7a (above left)
Round the Twist. Hand-pieced
and quilted cotton and cotton
blends; polyester batting,
59" x 76" (Nancy Halpern, 1976)

Plate 7b (below left)
Detail, *Round the Twist*

Plate 8 (above)
Wicked Lily. Machine-pieced
top, cotton blends, 72" x 72"
(Beth and Jeffrey Gutcheon,
1977). Photo courtesy of
the artists

Plate 9 (above)
Checquered Diamonds
Hand-pieced and hand-quilted
cotton and cotton blends,
56" x 56" (Ethel Klane, 1977)

Plate 10 (below)
Florescent Rag. Hand-appliquéd
and quilted cotton, 60" x 60"
(author, 1977)

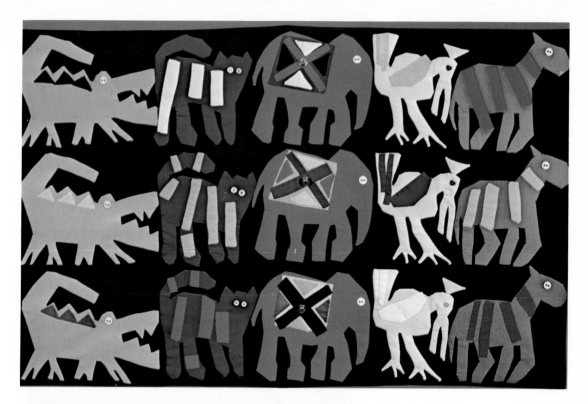

Plate 11 (above)
Animal Banner. Hand-appliquéd
cotton poplin, 24″ x 36″
(Jane Burke, 1975)

Plate 12 (below)
Brill. Machine-pieced,
hand-appliquéd, hand-quilted,
72″ x 92″ (Nancy Crow, 1977;
quilted by Velma Brill)

Plate 13 (above left)
Detail, *Night Sky 1.* (author)

Plate 14a (below left)
Night Sky 2. Hand-pieced and
hand-quilted cotton, satin, and
velveteen; polyester batting,
88″ x 96″ (author, 1976-1977)
Collection of
Joan Kaufmann-Wolfson

Plate 14b (right)
Detail, *Night Sky 2*

Plate 15 a (above)
*Bedloe's Island
Pavement Quilt*
Hand- and machine-pieced,
hand-quilted cottons,
woolens, and blends,
76'' x 88'' (author,1975)

Plate 15b (below)
Detail, *Bedloe's Island
Pavement Quilt*

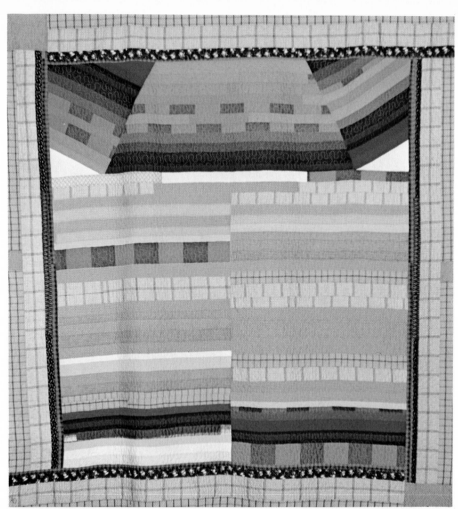

Plate 16a (above)
Dialogue
Machine-pieced and
machine-quilted cotton
and cotton blends,
84" x 100"
(Radka Donnell, 1975;
quilted by
Claire Mielke)

Plate 16b (below)
Detail, *Dialogue*

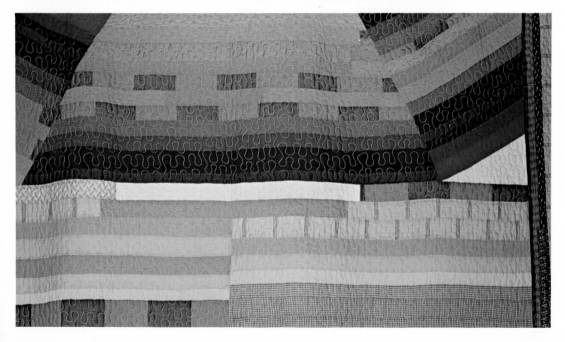

Plate 17 (above)
Incarnation. Machine-pieced,
hand-quilted cotton blends;
polyester batting, 96" x 96"
(Nancy Crow, 1976; quilted by
the Amish). Photo courtesy
of the artist

Plate 18 (below)
Mandala. Machine-pieced,
hand-quilted cotton blends;
polyester batting, 70" x 70"
(Beth Gutcheon, 1976)
Photo courtesy of the artist

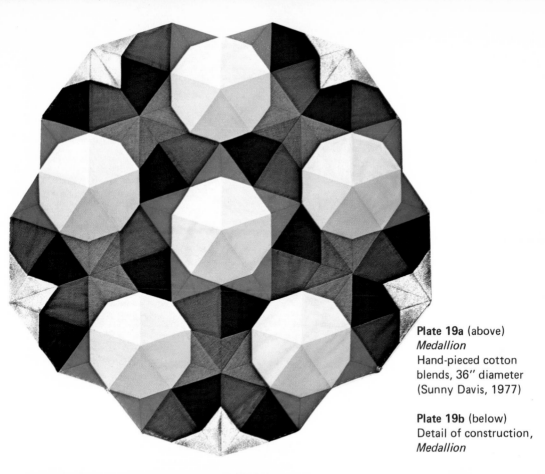

Plate 19a (above)
Medallion
Hand-pieced cotton
blends, 36″ diameter
(Sunny Davis, 1977)

Plate 19b (below)
Detail of construction,
Medallion

Plate 20 (left)
Seminole-style patchwork shirt. (Patchwork by the author; shirt by Judith James, 1976)

Plate 21 (below)
Seminole-style patchwork pillows. Machine-pieced cotton blends, 22″ x 22″ (author, 1976)

abstract composition came about in response to the somewhat sinister visual "feel" of the polished navy blue cotton fabric (see Fig. 5-11 and Plate 13). Wind-blown, cloudlike shapes move around the surface reflecting light in constantly shifting variations. The batting used in this quilt is made of dacron, which permits the 4-in. (10-cm) wide unquilted areas to contrast effectively with the ¼-in. (6-mm) and ½-in. (1.3-cm) intervals in the quilted sections. All of the quilting was done with dark blue thread.

Sas Colby has combined pieced work with whole-cloth blocks in "Figures with Log Cabin Squares" (Fig. 5-27). The juxtaposition of the traditional Log Cabin form and the nude female figure studies shows how two otherwise unrelated, two-dimensional expressions can be joined harmoniously in one quilt. The figures were first drawn by machine, with hand-stitched shading then added to further define their features. Hand quilting by Joan North works to emphasize the implied volume of each figure within the solid blocks.

Figure 5-27 *Figures with Log Cabin Squares*, by Sas Colby. Quilting by Joan North, 1975. Machine-drawn figures with hand-stitched shading. Machine pieced, hand quilted, 7' x 7'. Photo courtesy of the artist.

Historically, rich detail and exquisite workmanship were hallmarks of the all-white quilt. Elizabeth Gurrier carries on this tradition in such innovative pieces as "Angel Panel" (Fig. 5-28). The sculptural possibilities of fabric are here explored as the quilted surface forms itself into an outer garment for the figure (recalling elaborately quilted clothing of centuries past). Loose stuffing gives form to the face, hands, and feet, as well as to the tubular wings that dominate the panel. Hand and machine quilting and embroidery decorate the surfaces, lending a highly elegant character to the unbleached muslin fabric.

Figure 5-28 *Angel Panel*, by Elizabeth Gurrier, 1977. Hand embroidered face, machine quilting; unbleached muslin; stuffing, 67" x 24". Photo courtest of the artist, Photo by Robert Raiche.

"Women's Circle" (Figs. 5-29 and 5-30) is a rather good-humored, tongue-in-cheek reinvention of the popular "kaleidoscope" choreography of the Busby Berkeley musical. Twelve slightly obese ladies, spreading their arms in unison to form a lacy fringe to the quilt, revolve around a nest of similarly mohair-encircled and somewhat tired looking faces, each hand embroidered. Fine contour quilting by machine defines the breasts, belly, and thighs of each figure, and these last group around the center to form a sunflowerlike image. The fun and enjoyment the quiltmaker has experienced in manipulating the fabric and the forms is reflected in the "sense" of the piece.

Figure 5-29 *Women's Circle*, by Elizabeth Gurrier, 1976. Hand embroidered faces, machine quilting; unbleached muslin, mohair, stuffing. 112" diameter. Photo courtesy of the artist, Photo by Robert Raiche.

Figure 5-30   Detail, *Women's Circle.*

6 The Quilt

Because it can be folded and pleated and smoothed flat, and because it is soft and can provide warmth and because it can be laundered, the quilt has been regarded over many centuries as a functional bedroom furnishing. That the surface of the quilt could also be highly decorative and thus provide an enriching visual experience as well was recognized early on, but its practical use as a bedcovering was never out of mind. So it remains, for the most part, into the late twentieth century, although a growing acceptance of the quilt as art object, whole unto itself and relieved of any functional obligations, augurs well for an expressive medium heretofore viewed narrowly as "folksy" and "domestic."

What is a quilt? As the definition of "quilting" refers to the process of stitching through layers of fabric to secure them as one, and is a label for the stitches themselves, it is clear then that a quilt is a textile or fiber sandwich of two or more layers held together by those same hand or machine "quilting" stitches. To complete the definition, it must be said that the quilt is an object that has two outer surfaces and (with few exceptions) an inner filling or batting, with finished edges enclosing that filling and defining the dimensions of the piece. To elaborate upon this definition, we can add that a quilt usually has a front and back, each distinct from the other as surfaces, and that it is on the front surface (generally) that a flat, two-dimensional or stuffed, low-relief pattern or design or composition is worked out. And an even fuller description may be had by listing the physical characteristics of quilts: their softness, pliability, and tactile appeal.

From a historical point of view, this definition of the quilt would be incomplete without reference to the quilt's possible function as bedcovering and body insulation, for in the making of the quilt the needleworker intended her product for family use. More often than not, size was predetermined by the dimensions of the bedstead that would ultimately receive the quilt; and this initial restriction would furnish an additional challenge in designing the pattern to conform to those dimensions, particularly if the pattern was a traditional block. Questions of balance, rhythm, symmetry, and visual "weight" as well as color would have to be resolved while keeping in mind the final disposition of the quilt.

The contemporary quiltmaker who intends to use his or her quilt as bedcovering must also pay heed to these same considerations and to the practical limitations imposed by bed size, fabric and batting launderability, and the like. Whether one is adapting a traditional pattern or creating an original surface, attention must be paid to the design challenges presented by such restrictions. Likewise for the quiltmaker designing for a particular wall in a particular room: all formal elements of the quilt surface must take into account the limitations imposed by the setting in which it is to be hung.

When no functional demands are to be made of the quilt and its design and construction are to be experienced as building processes complete unto themselves, the quiltmaker need feel no formal design or dimensional restrictions other than those that he himself imposes or that are imposed by the design itself as it grows or by the materials employed. A (hypothetical) textile sandwich that happens to be round, made of sheer fabric and filled with colored batting, and quilted by machine with nylon thread, is no less a quilt because of the unorthodox materials employed or because it would not fit a conventional bed. In both form and technique it adapts and extends the tradition and creates a link in the chain of aesthetic development of the quilt as art object.

The matter of quilt size is, for the most part, an offshoot of the intended function of the piece. If a quilt is being planned for use on a bed, its dimensions should conform (approximately) to the size of the bed and should take into account the presence or absence of head- and footboards, as well as the special structural features of waterbeds and platform beds. Standard mattress sizes are as follows:

Crib: 27" × 50" (.70 m × 1.30 m)
Twin: 39" × 75" (1 m × 1.95 m)
Double: 54" × 75" (1.40 m × 1.95 m)
Queen: 60" × 80" (1.50 m × 2.10 m)
King: 72" × 80" (1.85 m × 2.10 m)

Note that these are the dimensions of the top of the mattress and do not include the mattress and boxspring depth, which should enter into size considerations. Depending on how much you wish to cover, this could add from 6 in. to 15 in. (15 cm to 38 cm) or more all around the standard mattress measurement.

The size of a wall quilt will be dictated by the size of the space within which it will hang. More often than not, however, this space size will be variable, and no standard measurements can be suggested. Size will just as likely be suggested by the design itself. This power of the image to dictate the ultimate dimensions of the quilt should not be overlooked. Both with traditional patterns, their adaptations and variations, as well as with original repeat block or free-form designs, the size of the block units (if any) or of other compositional elements must be taken into account in determining size.

For example, a block pattern drafted as a 15-in. (38-cm) square, grouped four blocks by four, would total 60 in. by 60 in. (150 cm by 150 cm). In order to function as a spread on a queen-size bed, the patterned area would have to be enlarged by adding at least one more row of blocks, for a total pieced area of 60 in. by 75 in. (150 cm by 175 cm), and then a 15-in. (38-cm) border or series of borders to expand the total size to about 90 in. by 105 in. (2.30 m by 2.65 m). An alternative would be to enlarge the size of the blocks themselves to 20 in. (51 cm), for a total pieced area of 80 in. by 80 in. (2.15 m by 2.15 m), and then to add a 10-in. (25.5-cm) border all around for a final size of 100 in. by 100 in. (2.50 m by 2.50 m). Keep in mind, however, that dramatically enlarging a block design that is very simple geometrically with only a small number of unit pieces, such as the traditional Variable Star pattern (Fig. 3-2a), can produce an awkward, oversized image. Conversely, enlarging an intricate design with many unit pieces can help to clarify the total visual impact of the surface while simplifying the sewing process as well.

In embarking on the making of a quilt, start by choosing the tentative size, either based on practical needs or on an arbitrary judgment suggested simply by how large or small you wish to work. Go on from there on paper to adapt and alter the pattern, and the size if need be, until the plan reflects your idea of what the quilt should look like.

ESTIMATING YARDAGE

Knowing exactly how much fabric you will need for a given project, especially a large quilt, can save you much time and unnecessary anxiety, particularly when you're working with a limited color scheme and range of fabrics. Although I don't always calculate yardages while planning a quilt (in a multicolored or "scrapbag" type of quilt, for example, it would be impractical to do so), I sometimes find it helpful to figure approximate amounts, particularly if I want to know if I have enough of a fabric on hand.

"Educated" guessing can be fairly dependable in this regard, providing you've had enough quiltmaking experience to back up that judgment. I usually opt for buying a bit more fabric than my "educated" guess indicates; and in the long run this can prove to be a costly approach, although leftover fabrics do, in time, find their way into another quilt or two.

If you wish to be accurate, and I urge you to be so in *all* facets of quiltmaking, you may follow one of two approaches in estimating yardage. In either case, you must first draft and cut all templates for your quilt, labeling each A, B, C, D, and so on, and indicating on each template the total number of pieces of that size needed in each color of fabric. Listing the total number you'll be cutting on each respective template keeps the appropriate figures at hand for ready reference.

Having multiplied and/or added your way to determining how many pieces of each size you'll need, you can then calculate the yardage. Determine how many pieces of a particular template (including seam allowances) can be laid out across a given width of fabric. For example, a 4-in. (10-cm) square template prepared for machine sewing (it will include seam allowances) can be laid across a 36-in. (90-cm) width of fabric nine times and eleven times across a 45-in. (115-cm) width. If you need 212 of those squares, you will need about 3 yd (2.75 m) of the 36-in. wide fabric or about 2¼ yd (2.10 m) of 45-in. (115-cm) fabric. You have divided the total number needed (212) by the amount of pieces in one width of fabric (9 or 11, in this case), then multiplied that result by 4 (or 10) to find the total in inches (or centimeters) needed. You then convert to yards (or meters), adding a bit extra to allow for any cutting errors you might make.

For appliqué, first determine the dimensions of the square area occupied by the appliqué shape, including seam allowances, and go on from there to calculate your amounts.

A second method of estimating yardage relies in great measure on your willingness to call forth from your subconscious memory those high school geometry formulas you thought would never find a practical application in your later everyday life. Besides rediscovering that they do work, you'll find that the discipline required to follow the formulas through is a fitting complement to the discipline with which you should approach all of the quilt-making processes.

The formulas most often used are the following:

Area of a square = s^2 (side times itself)
Area of a rectangle = base $\times$ height
Area of a triangle = $\frac{1}{2}$ (base $\times$ height)
Area of a rhomboid = base $\times$ height

These will allow you to find the square area of each template piece; this you'll need to know in order to determine the estimated yardage using this formula:*

$$\frac{\text{Area of the piece (including seam allowances)} \times \text{the number of pieces}}{\text{usable width of the fabric (in in. or cm)}} = \frac{\text{total length}}{\text{needed}}$$

For example, let's say that you need 310 triangles of a certain color. The finished size of the triangle will be 3 in. by 3 in. (7.5 cm by 7.5 cm) at the 90-degree angle, or just about 4 in. by 4 in. (10 cm by 10 cm) including seam allowances. The area, $\frac{1}{2}(4\times4)$ is 8 sq. in. (50 sq. cm). That area multiplied by 310 totals 2,480 sq. in. (15,500 sq. cm). Since eleven 4-in. triangles can be placed on a 45-in. width of fabric, leaving 1 in. extra, the *usable* width is 44 in. (115 cm). The total length needed in this case is 56 in. (140 cm), which is just a bit

*Beth Gutcheon, *The Perfect Patchwork Primer* (Baltimore, Md.: Penguin Books, Inc., 1974), p. 136. Used with permission of Jeffrey Gutcheon.

more than 1½ yd (1.40 m). Rounding the total upward to the nearest quarter-yard to account for any errors or inaccuracies in placement and cutting, we arrive at a total of 1¾ yd (1.60 m).

Yardages for borders and lattice can also be estimated using either of these methods. Calculations for borders will be influenced by whether you decide to piece the borders at their mid-points, or cut their full lengths from the goods. In the latter case, it is likely that you will have fabric left over, particularly if the borders are relatively narrow. If, however, you are cutting smaller pieces for the design in the same fabric, these can often be accommodated in the extra yardage after the borders have been marked and cut.

I'm always buying fabric, usually long before I have any idea of how it will be used in a quilt. I enjoy having a wide selection of solid and printed fabrics on hand with which to plan designs and/or fumble for inspiration. Depending on how much I'm attracted to a particular material and how much my budget will allow, I usually buy anywhere from ½ to 2 yd (0.50 m to 2 m) of a piece. When I do get down to planning a quilt, being able to estimate yardage allows me to determine which fabrics from my stock will find their way into the project. If I don't have enough of a preferred color and find that I can't obtain more, I either substitute a similar fabric or alter the color plan for the quilt. I don't think that it pays creatively to be inflexible when it comes to choosing fabric colors for a piece. The rich and varied body of quilt design is proof enough that scores of color variations, even within the same pattern, can create visually dazzling surfaces of incomparable beauty.

THE SET

The "set" refers to the manner in which geometric blocks in a quilt—whether they are pieced, appliquéd, or whole-cloth—are put together to form the whole surface. There are several conventional ways of setting blocks.

Lattice strips have been used widely in joining quilt blocks to form a top. These are narrow, rectangular strips sewn between the blocks and between rows of blocks to join them as one. Lattice can be unbroken bands of printed or solid color, or they can be separated by contrasting squares at their intersections (Fig. 6-1). Lattice strips serve to unite block designs and colors that might otherwise fail to work harmoniously, allowing each block to maintain its separate identity. At the same time, it increases the size of the quilt top.

In straight up-and-down lattice, two templates will be needed: a rectangular template as long as the side of the blocks being set, and a square template equal to the width of the lattice band. This square "intersection" should be used even if the lattice is a solid, unbroken color, as it assures that blocks will be aligned both horizontally and vertically.

When setting blocks together with lattice, treat the construction of the top in the same way you treat the construction of a single block. Sew blocks together in rows according to your quilt plan, alternating strips of lattice with the blocks (Fig. 6-1). Between rows of blocks, sew complete rows of lattice bands with square intersections, carefully joining corners of blocks with the corners of the square intersections.

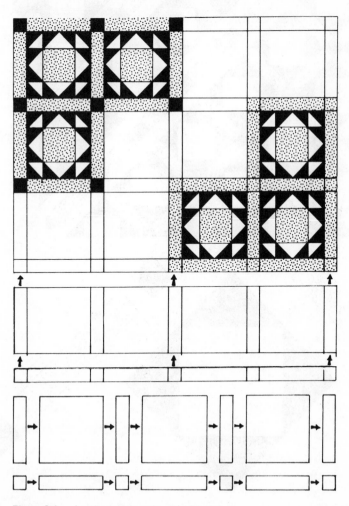

Figure 6-1 *Lattice construction.* Horizontal.

Figure 6-2   *Lattice construction.* Diagonal.

When setting blocks together with lattice on the diagonal of the surface, two additional triangular templates will be needed. One will be one-half the size of the intersection square, and the other will be one-fourth the size of the square (Fig. 6-2).

Pieced or appliqué blocks may be set together with alternate "whole-cloth" blocks, an arrangement that increases the ground surface of the quilt top design and that separates the blocks, thus allowing each to maintain its original identity. These whole-cloth sets can be arranged parallel to the sides of the quilt top, in straight up-and-down and side-to-side rows or diagonally to the sides of the quilt top. In this case triangular sections of the block must be used to complete the square or rectangular format at the edges and corners of the pattern (Fig. 6-3). Traditionally, these block settings have provided plain fields for fancy quilting.

Straight block-to-block setting provides the most potential for creating accidental or multiple patterns within a single pieced or appliqué design. Radically different variations on the same traditional pattern can be effected by changing light and dark color

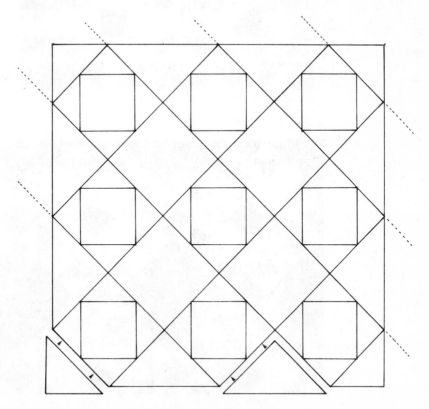

Figure 6-3 *Alternate whole-cloth set.* Pieced blocks are sewn with alternate squares and triangles in diagonal rows.

placement within the blocks, thus altering the center of focus in the design. Blocks may be divided and rearranged to form completely new designs. They may be set in straight rows, or arranged on diagonals (see Fig. 6-4), or alternated with different block designs to create original abstract surfaces. The block for the quilt "Razzle Dazzle" (Plate 2), for example, was set in rows horizontally and

Figure 6-4   Horizontal and diagonal sets of the same block pattern.

Figure 6-5 *Razzle Dazzle* block. The sense of the pattern is changed by giving the block a quarter turn.

vertically. When that same block is given a one-quarter turn (Fig. 6-5) the sense of the design is changed dramatically; and when it is arranged on the diagonal within the rectangular format, a new surface emerges (Fig. 6-6). Further examples of block-to-block sets may be seen in Figs. 6-9 and 6-10.

Figure 6-6 *Razzle Dazzle variation.* Diagonal arrangement of the block shown in Figure 3-39.

BORDERS

The border of a quilt encloses the body of the design, usually defining the outer dimensions of the piece but sometimes separating compositional elements within the patterned areas. It is made up of relatively long, narrow bands of whole cloth or of pieced or appliquéd fabric, joining at right angles to the quilt body.

The border usually serves to add emphasis to the main center of interest in the quilt. It prevents allover repeated unit designs from seemingly running off out of the two-dimensional plane of the quilt. It confines visually active designs and gives the viewer some degree of relief from complex color arrangements. While providing a handy means for achieving surface balance, it can give needed "weight" to particularly subtle design areas.

Although the border is by no means a necessary element in the design of a quilt surface, it can be the critical factor in establishing a total overall design unity, and its use should be considered as carefully as any other part of the design.

The pieced border can serve to introduce a variation of the pieced design that it encloses, or it can serve to extend the main design by carrying a geometric element of the pattern out toward the edges of the quilt (Fig. 6-7). It may also introduce a completely new design element to the surface, as in "Roman Stripe Composition Quilt"

Figure 6-7 *Border designs.* Elements of the block patterns are used as framework.

(Plates 5a and 5b) in which an ordered, symmetrical Roman Stripe border surrounds an abstract geometric composition.

Appliquéd borders can likewise help to unify an appliqué surface and can be used as well to contrast with and soften the hard-edged quality of a geometric pieced quilt. The border has been used as a setting for panoramic pictorial histories in appliqué, as well as for horticultural displays of breath-taking complexity; and it continues to provide a design challenge for the contemporary quiltmaker as well.

Figure 6-8   Border and corner arrangement of *Razzle Dazzle.*

The whole-cloth border is perhaps the most common type. In addition to enclosing the patterned areas of the quilt and re-organizing or unifying the color theme, it also provides a plain field in which emphasis can be placed on elaborate quilting designs.

Whenever possible, plan for the border(s) when planning the quilt as a whole. This will allow you to determine the ultimate size of the quilt as well as the additional yardage of a color or colors you'll need. Keep in mind in the planning stage that the border can also provide an outlet for creative expression: it can be shaped as well as straight sided, patterned as well as plain (Fig. 6-8).

Figure 6-9 shows a simple, "butted" border and the sequence in which the border sections are attached. First, determine the outer measurements of the main section of the quilt. If, for example, this measures 60½ in. by 70½ in. (151 cm by 176 cm), including seam allowances, and the border is to finish 6 in. (15 cm) wide, two border strips must be cut 6½ in. by 70½ in. (16 cm by 176 cm), and two others 6½ in. by 72½ in. (16 cm by 181 cm). Two borders are pinned and sewn to corresponding opposite sides, and then the remaining two are attached in turn.

Multiple borders are put on in the same way, one at a time, so that each border is completed before the next is sewn. "Florescent Rag" (Plate 10) is a good example.

Borders may be broken at corners with contrasting colors, as in "Bedloe's Island Pavement Quilt" (Plates 15a and 15b) and "Night Sky 2" (Plate 14a). In this instance, border strips are cut to correspond to the measurements of the sides of the body of the quilt. Visualize a design of twenty blocks measuring 48½ in. by 60½ in. (123 cm by 151 cm) to which a 9-in. (23-cm) border with contrasting corners is to be sewn. Two border strips, each 9½ in. by 60½ in. (24 cm by 151 cm) including seam allowances are pinned and sewn to the long sides of the design (as in Fig. 6-10). Corner squares measuring 9½ in. by 9½ in. (24 cm by 24 cm) are sewn to the ends of the two remaining strips, and these last border sides are then pinned and sewn to the body of the quilt. Care should be taken as in all piecing that points match carefully and that sewing is faithful to the ¼-in. (6-mm) seam allowance.

It is not necessary to have yardage available in lengths that will accommodate the full span of border strips. Long borders can be pieced by seaming at the halfway point (Fig. 6-9), and this can be a fabric-saving advantage with narrow border widths in particular. When piecing the border to attain the desired length, sew sections together by machine; and in this case only press the seam allowances open, so that the seam will be as inconspicuous as possible.

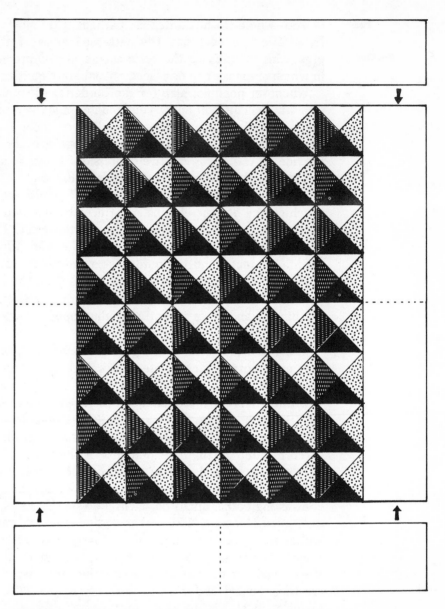

Figure 6-9 *Solid butted border.* Dotted lines indicate seams.

When cutting border strips from fabric, I usually measure the widths of the strips from the selvage, if this is relatively straight, or from a straight line ruled in pencil on the fabric. When hand-piecing the borders to the quilt, the sewing line must be marked as in all hand piecing. Measure the desired widths from the straight edge of the fabric, indicating both the sewing and cutting lines. When machine sewing, you need mark only the cutting line, including seam allowance in each border measurement.

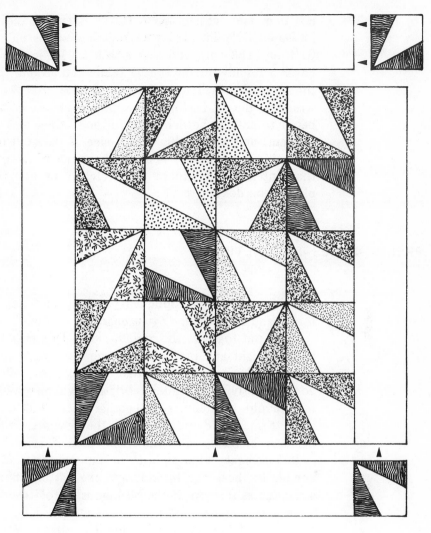

Figure 6-10   *Butted border with contrasting corners.*

It is extremely important in preparing borders for the quilt that you plan their measurements to correspond to the dimensions of the quilt as you had planned them at the outset. In working any quilt design, pieced patterns in particular, there is usually some stretching of fabric or some gathering here and there if thread slack is pulled a little too tightly in sewing. Such inconsistencies can alter the outer dimensions of the patterned area by as much as 1 in. (2.5 cm) and sometimes more, either increasing or decreasing the original measurements. If you measure the lengths of the sides to which you are going to attach borders and then cut border lengths to correspond, it is quite likely that you may be cutting more or less than you actually need. If, for example, the side should have measured 60½ in. (151 cm) including seams but finished at about 61¼ in. (153 cm), and you attach a 61¼-in. border, you will discover a fullness in the border fabric and around the outer edges of the quilt that will not smooth out and that will cause excessive wrinkling during basting and quilting. In this instance, it would be better to cut the border strips to the planned size (here, 60½ in. or 151 cm) and attach this to the edge of the quilt top, easing excess fabric in as the pinning is done. If the side of the quilt top is shorter than intended, it should be stretched to accommodate the full planned border length.

PRELIMINARIES TO QUILTING

You have pieced or appliquéd your top and attached the borders, if any, and are now ready to prepare for quilting.

First, put together the quilt backing. This may be any fabric that is lightweight and preferably of the same fiber content as the top of the quilt. Bear in mind that your quilting will not show up as conspicuously on a printed fabric as it will on a solid. A large project may require that you seam together several widths of yardage. There is no firm rule dictating where the seams should lie; they must, however, be neatly sewn and crisply pressed, seams open.

If a separate binding is to be put on the quilt after quilting is completed, both the backing and the batting should be cut to the same size as the top. If the backing is to fold over the top edge and serve as a binding, it should be cut at least 1 in. (2.5 cm) larger all around than the top and batting. Conversely, if the top edge is to fold over the back of the quilt, the backing and batting should be cut 1 in. smaller all around.

Proceed to sandwich the layers as described in Chap. 5, and baste as indicated in Fig. 5-15.

Complete and proper basting assures you that the three layers of the quilt will not shift while the quilting is done. It also helps to prevent any pulling or tearing of the batting, particularly if it is not synthetic.

Marking the quilting design can be done either before the three layers are basted together, or after, as the quilting proceeds. Since on a large quilt the marking can be a very time-consuming process, I suggest marking an area at a time and then quilting it. I have taken to marking the quilt section-by-section while it is stretched in the hoop; this allows for fairly uniform measurements. The fact that the three layers are stretched in mid-air, so to speak, rather than spread out on a hard surface helps to prevent one from pressing down too hard with the pencil.

BINDING

The binding encloses the raw edges of the quilt sandwich, adding the "finish" to the piece. As mentioned before, a quilt can be self-binding; that is, either the top or back edge is brought over to the reverse side, hemmed, and hand stitched in place. It is the quickest way to bind.

The separate binding is an additional strip of fabric sewn all around the outside edge of the quilt. In the long run, and from a practical standpoint, it is the most efficient means to bind. Anyone who has studied the effects of time and wear on a quilt knows that the binding is one of the first places to show signs of deterioration. A separate binding allows you to replace worn fabric early on, with little or no change to the body of the quilt.

Binding strips should be cut about 1½ in. (3.8 cm) wide and may be pieced of any number of lengths of fabric, providing the seams are matched on the bias of the fabric and pressed open (Fig. 6-11). The binding itself, however, need not be cut on the bias of the fabric, unless it is being made to cover a curved or rounded edge. For example, only the binding sections at the four corners of "Night Sky 2" (Plate 14a) were cut on the bias.

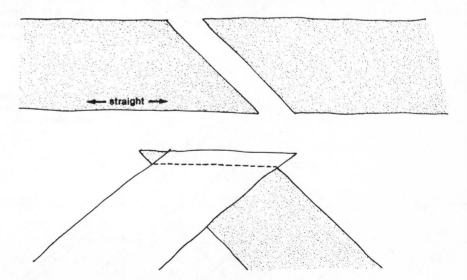

Figure 6-11 *Bias piecing of straight binding.*

Binding is attached to the quilt in the same way that borders are sewn on, working opposite sides in sequence. The binding is first pinned to the trimmed edge of the quilt and sewn in place by hand or machine, taking a ¼-in. (6-mm) to ⅜-in. (1-cm) seam. Care should be taken that any pieced points in the design that reach the edge of the quilt meet the binding precisely. The binding is then folded over the back and a final hem is folded under. If the binding was sewn to the top by machine, this line of stitching should be hidden on the back side by the binding. The folded binding is pinned in place all around the back of the quilt, corners are folded neatly, and a final blindstitch or overcast stitch secures it to the backing (see Figs. 6-12 to 6-15).

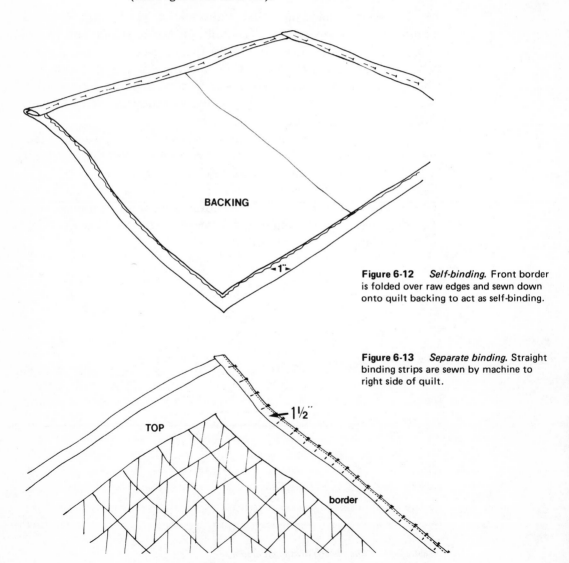

BACKING

Figure 6-12   *Self-binding.* Front border is folded over raw edges and sewn down onto quilt backing to act as self-binding.

Figure 6-13   *Separate binding.* Straight binding strips are sewn by machine to right side of quilt.

TOP

border

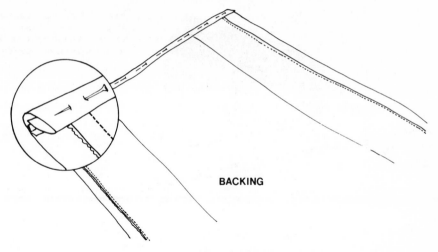

Figure 6-14 Binding is folded over raw edges of quilt and pinned in place on backing. Corners are folded neatly.

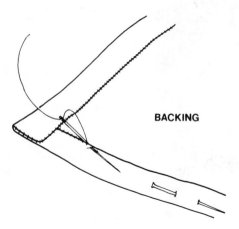

Figure 6-15 Using blind or overcast (shown here) appliqué stitches, binding is sewn to backing. Note corner completely enclosed.

A decorative piping may be inserted along the top edge of the binding, as in "Roman Stripe Composition Quilt" (see detail, Plate 5b). This is sometimes helpful in subtly carrying a strong color out to the edge of the quilt.

To add a piping, determine the width you wish exposed. For a ⅛-in. (3-mm) piping, cut a fabric strip ¼-in. larger than the *finished* width of the binding that you plan to sew on. Press the piping in half along its length, and baste the folded piping along the edges of the quilt, raw edge to raw edge (Fig. 6-16). Corners need only be overlapped. Once this is in place, proceed with applying the binding as described above.

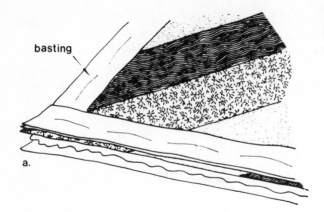

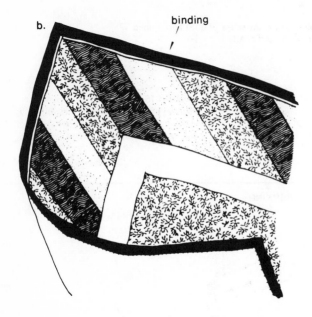

basting

a.

b.

binding

Figure 6-16 *Piping.* a. Folded piping strips are basted to raw edges of quilt. Corner is simply overlapped. b. Binding is sewn in place over piping.

SIGNING THE QUILT

Traditionally, most quilts have gone unsigned. In rare instances, the quiltmaker stitched his or her name and perhaps a date to the fabric, but in general the craft has remained an anonymous one.

I think that the decision to sign and date a quilt remains a personal one. I do think, however, that where quiltmaking is no longer primarily motivated by domestic or economic necessity, and where artistic intent encourages exploration of new forms and reinterpretations of familiar patterns, the quiltmaker should keep in mind that

110

knowledge of the provenance of any work of art can often be a key to understanding at least a part of what went into making it.

I have signed my quilts in several ways, sometimes on the front of the piece, sometimes on the back, in embroidery as well as in ink. Here again, there are no rules to follow, other than your own best judgment. Quite naturally, neatness of execution is of prime importance in this process as in all quiltmaking processes.

Cross-stitched or otherwise embroidered signatures by their nature go hand-in-hand with the textile surfaces of the quilt. Consult a good manual on embroidery for charted alphabets that you can vary to reflect your own personality or to complement the surface design of your quilt. I always sign my quilts after they're completed and usually attach fabric labels on the back identifying the title of the quilt (Figs. 6-17 and 6-18).

Figure 6-17   *Cross-stitched label.*

Figure 6-18   *Cross-stitched label.*

India ink may be used as well in signing your work. Keep in mind that the ink is permanent, and several trial runs on scrap fabric are advised before writing directly on the quilt. Better yet, labels such as that for "Elaborated Tangram" can be made and sewn in place on the back of the quilt (Fig. 6-19). The 1½ in. by 2½ in. (3.8 cm by 6.5 cm) label gives title, artist, and date, and here an empty space was enlivened with a sketch of my number 11 thimble.

If you plan to quilt your signature and date, remember that legibility will depend on how closely your quilting stitches are made. With a fairly lightweight fabric, such as the polished cotton blend in "Night Sky 1" (Fig. 6-20) used with polyester batting, you'll be able to quilt a bit closer than with cotton batting and all-cotton broadcloth; so in this case a quilted signature should work well.

Jane Burke found a unique way to sign her "Alphabet" coverlet. Her stylized self-portrait in the "J" block (Fig. 6-21), complete with striped quilt and stuffed doll, reflects the humorous spirit of the rest of the top and at the same time gives us a personal look at its maker.

Figure 6-19   *Hand-lettered label.*

Figure 6-20   *Hand-quilted signature and date.*

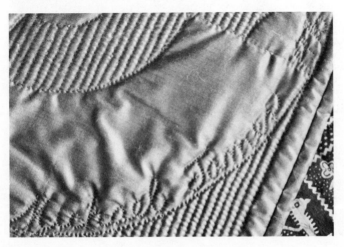

Figure 6-21 *Signature block.* Detail, *Janie's Alphabet.*

HANGING

If you plan to show your quilt on a wall, it's a good idea to provide a means to do so as you put the rest of the finishing touches on your piece.

A rod casing sewn to the top back of the quilt is probably best. It won't be visible when the quilt is hung or when it's used on a bed. For a quilt up to about 54 in. (140 cm) wide, a continuous casing, sewn from side to side, will be sufficient. For larger quilts, it's a good idea to apply the casing in two halves along the top back of the quilt (Fig. 6-23). This will allow the center of the hanging rod to be supported if necessary.

A 2½-in. (6.5-cm) wide casing is probably the most practical size. Cut strips of fabric 5½ in. (14 cm) wide, in lengths equal to the width of the quilt or to half the width if the casing is to be applied in two sections. Fold these in half, right sides together, and sew the bottom and long sides, taking a ¼-in. (6-mm) seam. Turn the whole casing inside out through the last open end, then turn the seam allowance inward and close the end (Fig. 6-22). This double-thickness casing is thus long-lasting and strong. Pin or baste the

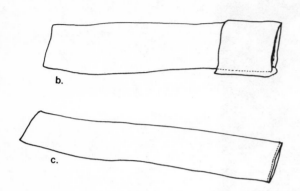

Figure 6-22 *Making a casing.* a. Two
sides of folded fabric are stitched right
sides together. b. Casing is turned right
side out. c. Raw edges are turned in and
end is stitched closed.

casing to the top back of the quilt so that the top edge of the casing
is about ½ in. (1.3 cm) from the top edge of the bound quilt. Using
an overcast appliqué stitch, sew the top and bottom edges of the
casing to the backing of the quilt, being careful not to sew through
to the right side. The casing finished in this way can accommodate
a metal or wooden rod or slat up to about 1¾ in. (4.5 cm) wide and
should not be apparent on the right side of the quilt.

Shaped quilts will present special hanging problems and must be
dealt with individually. "Night Sky 2," which has rounded corners,

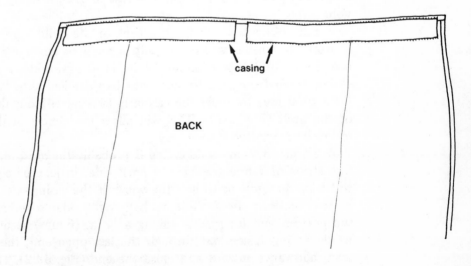

casing

BACK

Figure 6-23   Casing is stitched in place at top back of quilt.

was provided with a casing along the top back as described above. Small fabric loops were attached at the center and bottom of each top corner (Fig. 6-24), and through these pushpins are inserted into the wall to support the border panels.

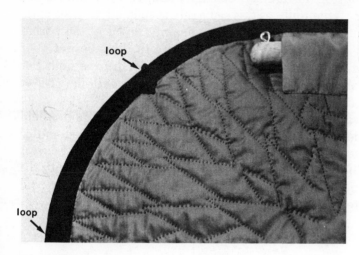

loop

loop

Figure 6-24   Casing for hanging attached to back top of *Night Sky 2*. Fabric loops attached for securing rounded corners.

TAKING CARE

At the beginning of Chapter 2 I noted that quilts were fragile by nature. Faced with washing a newly-finished quilt, it's a good time to think on that fact. Although your quilt should be pretty sturdy and will not have received very much wear in its short life, I think it's a good idea to get into habits of caring for your quilts that will follow through a lifetime.

If all of the fabrics are washable, and the quilt is used on a bed, a twice-yearly laundering will probably be necessary. Do it in the spring and fall, and choose breezy, dry, crystal-clear days. If yours is a wall quilt, washing once a year will keep it bright and clean, and at other regular intervals a gentle vacuuming of the surface with a nonbristle attachment will help to remove any accumulation of dust.

If you exhibit your quilts outside of your home or studio, be sure that they are scrupulously clean when they leave, and wash them, if necessary, on their return. I have exhibited quilts in climate-controlled environments from which they returned smelling and looking as fresh as the day they were first washed. On the other hand, some have returned from display bearing the battle scars of crowded opening-night receptions, countless hundreds of hands, and hurried dismantlings.

I always wash my quilts by hand, in a large sink or bathtub, depending on the size of the quilt. Water temperature should be lukewarm, and a mild liquid detergent may be used. Let the quilt soak for several minutes, then agitate gently. Rinse well, squeezing excess water out of the quilt as you empty and refill the tub. Do not twist or "wring" the quilt, as this can easily snap hand-sewn stitches. After rinsing, I place the quilt in the "spin-only" cycle of the washer to remove all excess water. As an alternative to this, the wet quilt may be rolled in absorbent toweling. If possible, dry the quilt flat or over two or three clotheslines, out of the sun, until dry. Never press a quilt.

Why not wash and dry in machines? At first, a new quilt would probably stand up to this well, particularly if it were pieced and/or quilted by machine. Over the long term, however, the extra wear afforded by the regular agitation of the machine, combined with the temptation to wash more frequently because of the ease, would shorten the life of the quilt considerably.

MORE CONTEMPORARY QUILTS

In presenting examples of innovative work in quiltmaking, I have attempted to complement some rather detailed explanations of the technical processes involved with examples of work that either change the whole form of the quilt as we've come to identify it, or at the least explore new horizons in surface imagery. Nearly all of the quiltmakers shown have grown and developed very gradually in their work. They have moved from the point where their first, somewhat tentative, stitches were taken in fabric to a level of technical control and design refinement that balance and support one another and indicate mastery of the form. As artists and craftsmen, they constantly seek to respond, through their materials, to new emotional and intellectual impressions that challenge, and thus reinforce, that mastery.

"Night Sky 2" (Plates 14a and 14b) by the author represents a response to just such a challenge. An earlier quilt (Fig. 5-11) interpreted the storm-tossed, moonlit night sky theme in line alone on a glazed fabric. "Night Sky 2" restates the theme in curved-seam piecing with the use of satin and velveteen in addition to cotton fabrics. The use of the heavier fabrics in a large piece that is entirely hand sewn necessitated adapting familiar sewing techniques to these particular materials.

The design of this quilt was worked out as the sewing proceeded. Each row of blocks was planned and cut at one sitting; colors and arrangements were based on that section already completed. Once each new row was completed and attached, the next would be prepared. Quilting follows the contour of each curved strip within the block, and at the corners quilted coronas enclose each circular "star." These same cone shapes are repeated in a meandering border design that recalls traditional feather patterns.

Multiple-color contrast studies are juxtaposed in "Bedloe's Island Pavement Quilt (Plates 15a and 15b). Each block is basically a color composition of sixteen squares; the blocks are held together as a whole by the solid yellow-orange lattice. Conventional crossbar quilting occupies the rather complex central area, and a continuous spiral pattern travels through the solid red borders. Like "Night Sky 2," the surface design evolved as comparisons and juxtapositions were made with completed areas.

With startling clarity, Radka Donnell lifts quiltmaking from the romanticism of the past and grounds it solidly in the reality of the present. The imposing blue monolith in her quilt "Dialogue" (Plates 16a and 16b) rests with architectural solidity on a support of variegated fabric strips that suggest a geological cross-section. The restrained use of white in the composition introduces a spatial element and simultaneously creates a great deal of surface tension. Tonal and value gradations within each of the major color areas provide some subtlety to an otherwise intense surface.

The straight lines and hard-edged quality of the composition contrast effectively with the meandering, jigsawlike quilting design superimposed on the pieced image. The machine quilting becomes an obvious part of the surface and in its regular "irregularity" reflects the interrupted order of the pieced design. A "dialogue" is set up; it speaks of postindustrial society.

Much of this same power is implicit in Nancy Crow's "Incarnation" (Plate 17), although the image develops out of different artistic and intellectual orientations. The quilt is one of a series based on liturgical themes. The spiritual mystery of transformation is represented in a highly complex surface alive with activity and the interplay of several design themes. The intensity of the red figures exploding in a predominantly green field forms an exciting contrast to the monochromatic value gradations that hold the surface together. A strip-piecing technique was employed here, greatly simplifying the construction of the top.

In "Mandala" (Plate 18) Beth Gutcheon has given order to a scrapbag-style pieced surface by concentrating stronger colors at the center and by superimposing a strong, well-integrated quilting design. The subtle coloration along the periphery of the quilt and the geometric fracturing of the surface bring to mind the fragility of fine crystal. Coincidentally, the three-dimensional openings in the quilt are intended as receptacles for geometric pieces of stained glass. Like all of the quilts shown in these pages, "Mandala" is a link in the chain connecting quiltmaking past and quiltmaking future.

Appendixes

APPENDIX A: ENGLISH PAPER PATCHWORK

Although this piecing technique is certainly not an exclusively English development, its widespread use in Great Britain over several centuries suggests the appellation. As a means to achieve nearly absolute precision in constructing pieced work, it is unchallenged. Mastery of the technique provides another useful tool for creative manipulation of the quilt surface.

Fabric is basted over notebook or a similar weight paper cut in the desired shape. Pieces thus prepared are stitched together with tiny "whip" stitches at the edges of the shapes. Once the entire piece has been worked, or a portion thereof, the paper is removed. The technique may be used with almost any geometric shape; it is particularly adaptable to constructing with hexagons, diamonds, and the like and can be used as a foundation for appliqué as well.

Prepare templates for the desired shapes as described in Chap. 3. These should not include seam allowance, as they are used to mark the paper foundations. Trace carefully around the template on a lightweight notebook or similar paper. If working with fabric heavier than the standard cotton broadcloth, it may be necessary to use a firmer paper; index cards will work well in this instance.

Cut the paper foundations as accurately as possible, using sharp, paper-cutting scissors. The precise outcome of the sewing process will depend in part on the care with which these are prepared.

Pin paper shapes to the fabric, placing these so as to allow an ample ¼-in. (6-mm) seam allowance when cutting each fabric piece (Fig. A-1). The shapes are arranged for cutting as with regular pieced work (see Fig. 3-24). It may be necessary with large shapes done in this method to thread-baste the paper to the fabric before cutting to prevent shifting. Cut ¼ in. larger all around the foundation shape.

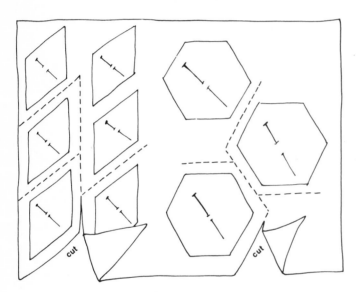

Figure A-1   Paper shapes are pinned to wrong side of fabric, and pieces are cut allowing for seams.

The fabric seam allowance is now carefully folded over the edge of the paper and basted in place (Fig. A-2a). Always begin at the widest angle of the piece. Narrow angles may require one or more extra folds, as in Fig. A-2b.

Shapes are sewn together by placing them right sides together, aligning the edges carefully, and whipstitching from one end of the seam to the other (Fig. A-3). A sharp is used, and thread should match as nearly as possible the darker of the fabrics being sewn. The needle is drawn through the very edges of the fabric, and stitches should be quite small and regular. If the edge of the paper foundation happens to be caught with needle and thread, it will simply tear away when the basting is removed and will not affect the sewn edge.

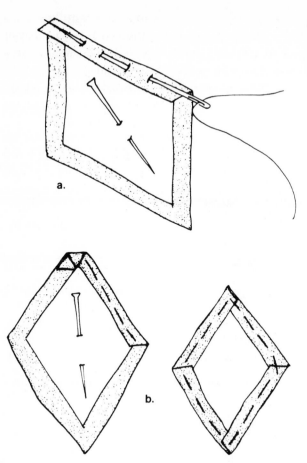

Figure A-2 a. Beginning at widest angle, seam allowance is basted over edge of paper. b. Corner is first folded down, parallel to edge of paper, and then over back, parallel to adjacent edge.

a.

b.

Figure A-3 Basted shapes are "whipped" together along edges with tiny stitches.

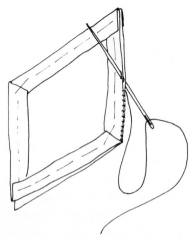

Once the piecing is completed, the basting is removed, all paper shapes are withdrawn, and the work may be pressed. If the pieced unit is to be appliquéd to a fabric foundation, the paper may be left inside until the appliqué is complete. The fabric backing is then cut away up to within ¼ in. (6 mm) of the stitched seam, and the paper is then removed.

Figure A-4 *English paper patchwork.* Detail of silk pillow by the author.

Figure A-5 *English paper patchwork.* Reverse side showing whipstitched seams.

Circles may be appliquéd accurately by basting the fabric over paper foundations as described above, easing the fabric seam allowance in small pleats over the edge of the paper. No clipping is necessary.

Portions of the quilt "Florescent Rag" (Plate 10) were prepared in this way. The round shape of the sun was basted over paper and appliquéd to the corona; the underlying fabric was then cut away and the paper removed. The body of the moon and the crescent shape were each basted over paper, then whipped together. The lunar circle was then appliquéd to the foundation, after which the backing was cut away and the paper removed. The concave inner curve of the crescent shape was clipped before basting over the edge of the paper. Each of the stars was pieced of six diamonds prepared over paper and then appliquéd, after which the paper was again removed.

A paper patchwork medallion (Plates 19a and 19b) using two angular shapes was worked by Sunny Davis as a class project in the technique. The strong light/dark and warm/cool color contrasts emphasize the spatial illusion created by the six shaded pyramids. Metallic fabric is used to create five gold clasps that contain the design and, by association, suggest the jewellike nature of the piece.

APPENDIX B: PRESSED PIECING—THE LOG CABIN

The term "log cabin," when used in regard to quilts, has gradually come to refer to both the technique as well as the design. The technique is more correctly referred to as *pressed piecing*, and it lends itself well to executing the strip designs whose historical origins are several hundreds of centuries older than the pioneer log cabin of early America.

The method presented here is a variation of the traditional one; it can be adapted and sewn several other ways, by machine as well as by hand.

Two templates will be needed. The template for the muslin foundation should be ½ in. (1.3 cm) larger all around than the planned measurement for the finished size. For instance, a 9-in. (23-cm) log cabin block will be constructed on a 10-in. (25.5-cm) muslin foundation. A square template will also be needed for the center piece. It must equal the width of the strips. For example, if the strips are 1½ in. (3.8 cm) wide, the center square will be 1½ in. by 1½ in. (including seam allowances).

Fabric strips for the design are cut from fabric yardage without the use of templates. Strips may be cut in any length, and the number of strips of one color that you'll need will depend on the size of the project. I've found 18-in. (46-cm) strips easy to manage for small projects, and they can be economically cut from ½ yd of fabric. Prepare an assortment of both light and dark fabric strips. The standard width of the strip in the finished piece is 1 in. (2.5 cm); this is variable, and it can be any multiple of the finished size of the block, depending on how wide you wish each band of color to be.

To cut the strips, first rule a straight line parallel to the selvage of the fabric, and cut carefully along this line to establish a straight edge from which the rest of the strips will be measured. It is critically important that both the sewing lines and the cutting lines be marked at precise measurements. For 1-in. finished strips, measure from the straight edge, marking intervals for the ¼-in. (6-mm) seam allowance, 1-in. (2.5-cm) strip, two ¼-in. seam allowances, a 1-in. strip, two seam allowances, and so forth. Cut the strips so that each is 1½ in. (3.8 cm) wide, including a seam allowance along each long side.

Mark the center of the muslin foundation by ruling diagonal lines from corner to corner of the fabric square. This will locate the center of the block. (Do not press to find the center, as this distorts the block size.) Place the center square, marked with the small template on its right side, and cut ¼ in. (6 mm) larger all around, at the center of the block. Align its corner points with the diagonal guidelines and baste in place (Fig. B-1).

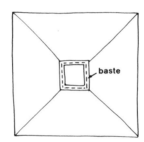

Figure B-1 *Log Cabin preparations.*

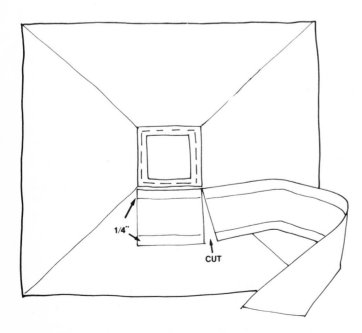

You are now ready to begin the piecing. Following the diagrams in Figs. B-3 and B-4 for either a diagonal light/dark arrangement or a quartered ("Courthouse Steps") arrangement, take a strip of fabric, place it alongside the center square so that its end is aligned with the edge of the square, and cut the strip so that it corresponds in length to the square (Fig. B-1).

Pin the first piece over the center square, right sides together, so that the seam allowances align (Fig. B-2). Sew with a running stitch along the line, sewing through the muslin foundation. Press flat.

In the diagonal arrangement, the second strip attached will be twice the length of the first; the third will be equal to the second; the fourth will be larger than the third, and so forth. Continue to cut the strips by "measuring" against those pieces already sewn. Be sure to press after each strip is sewn in place.

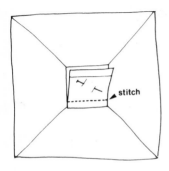
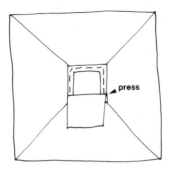

Figure B-2 *Log Cabin construction.*

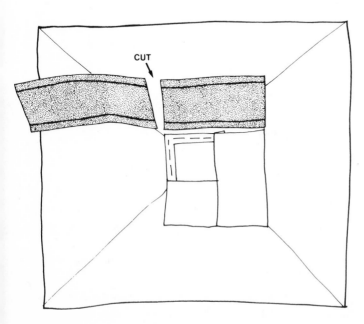

For the diagonal arrangement, always work consistently in the same direction, either clockwise or counterclockwise, sewing two lights, two darks, two lights, and so on. For the quartered arrangement, sew on facing sides, working two lights, then two darks, and so on.

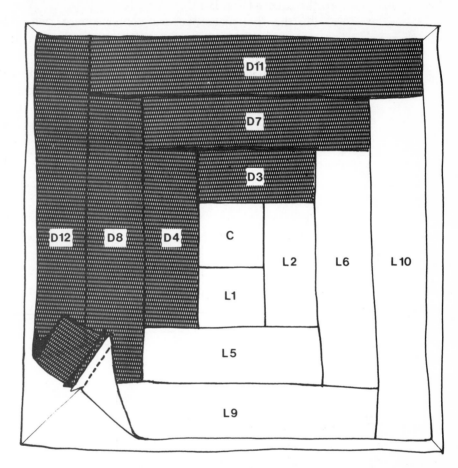

Figure B-3 *Diagonal Log Cabin arrangement.* Note that outer inch in each corner is not sewn through foundation.

Because this technique eliminates the need for using a series of templates for the strips, it saves time and minimizes any confusion as to which strip fits where. Bear in mind, however, that seam allowances must be very carefully aligned at all times and that the strips should always be parallel to the edges of the muslin foundation.

When the final outer strips are attached, the first inch and the last inch of each of these strips should be sewn to the ends of the

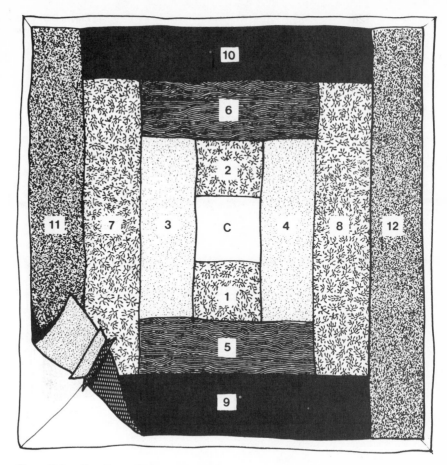

Figure B-4   *Courthouse Steps arrangement.*

previous strips, but not through the muslin foundation (see Figs. B-3 and B-4). This will leave ample room for joining blocks.

To join finished blocks, place right sides together, folding back the loose inch or so of muslin foundation to expose the seam allowances on the outer strips (Fig. B-5). Pin and sew with a running stitch as with regular piecing, and then press to one side. Lay one muslin backing flat, fold under ¼ in. (6 mm) to ½ in. (1.3 cm) of the other, and overlap (Fig. B-6). Sew to enclose all raw edges, using an overcast or a blindstitch as for appliqué.

The log cabin design, in one of its original applications as mummy wrapping, is revived by Sharon McKain in "Self-Portrait as Sarcophagus" (Fig. B-7). The blocks become very important decorative elements within the context of this highly symbolic surface.

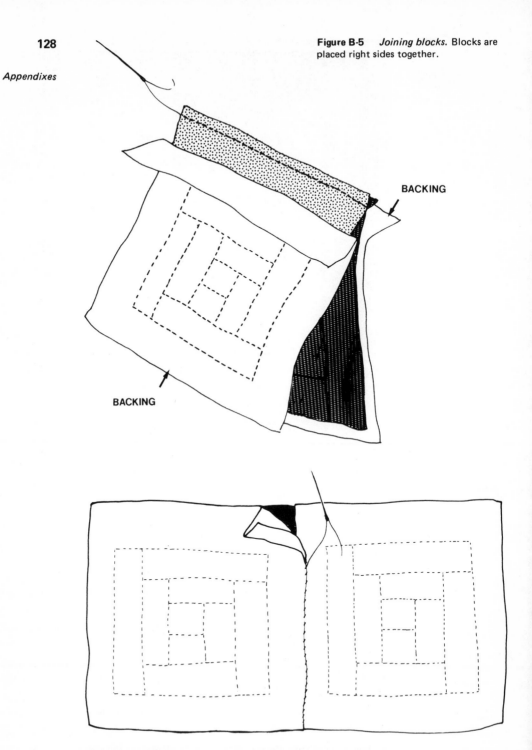

Figure B-5 *Joining blocks.* Blocks are placed right sides together.

BACKING

BACKING

Figure B-6 *Finishing Log Cabin.* Edges of the foundation are overlapped and become the backing of the spread.

Figure B-7 *Self-Portrait as Sarcophagus*, by Sharon McKain, 1975. Machine pieced, appliqué, log cabin; machine quilting, 6' x 10'. Collection of Robert Craft. Photo by Lizzy MacDonald, courtesy of the artist.

APPENDIX C: THE TECHNIQUE OF THE SEMINOLES

Pieced work and appliqué have been an important part of ethnic and regional costume ever since man first realized the decorative possibilities of salvaging worn clothing by repairing it with bits of cloth. In many cultures, patchwork has become the standard for ceremonial dress fabrics. Such is the case with the Seminole Indians of Florida, whose pride in their heritage is displayed in the intricate designs of their pieced garments.

The technique for creating "Seminole-style" patchwork can be described most effectively as *strip* piecing. Strips of fabric of varying widths are sewn together by machine. These are then cut into sections and resewn in different ways to arrive at any number of pieced arrangements. The technique is highly adaptable and can be used in making quilts as well as smaller furnishings and clothing. Design variations are limitless.

All cotton fabric is once again the easiest to handle with this technique, producing very crisp seams when pressed. This is an important consideration especially when working with very narrow strips. If the technique is being adapted for use in clothing, however, a broadcloth blend of 65 percent polyester and 35 percent cotton will be easiest to care for.

Always cut strips for Seminole patchwork on the straight grain of the fabric, that is, parallel to the selvage. This will minimize any stretch, while at the same time it will facilitate cutting and give greater consistency in strip width measurements. It is extremely difficult to estimate the total length of stripping of any one color that will be needed to execute a given design. Experience with the technique during what you might call an "apprenticeship" will help you to eventually make estimates based on the type of design you wish to do. I have found that for many of the most intricate designs, one needs at the outset up to three times as much length in stripping as the eventual length of the finished design. Naturally, the smaller the scale of the design, the greater the amount of fabric that will be taken up as seam allowance relative to the final design.

Press fabric before marking and cutting. Only the cutting lines need be marked on the fabric; the strips are measured to include seam allowance. For instance, if you wish the finished size of a square unit within a design to be 1 in. (2.5 cm), you must cut the strip 1½ in. (3.8 cm) wide. The addition of ½ in. (1.3 cm) to allow for ¼-in. (6-mm) seam allowances must be followed consistently through all planning and measuring. Mark the cutting lines by measuring from a straight raw edge (ruled out beforehand) or from the selvage if this is perfectly straight.

A cotton-covered polyester thread will work well at the machine for this technique. Sew strips together, taking about twelve stitches to the inch. Carefully press seams open; the straightness and crispness of the seam will determine the accuracy with which the actual design is formed.

Once the strips have been sewn together, the cutting for the actual design is done. Repeat units, which can be either squares, rectangles, rhomboids, or triangles, are marked with ruler and pencil directly on the sewn strips, taking care always to include proper seam allowance. The cut units are then resewn to form the desired pattern and finally pressed.

Study the diagrams for the construction of the representative designs illustrated here (Figs. C-1 through C-4). Keep in mind that in sewing by machine, you must be scrupulously faithful to the seam allowance if all points in the design are to match as intended. Notice that in some of the designs there is considerable waste of fabric as the strips are cut and resewn. Note also that the traditional approach to joining rows of pattern has been to set these between single or multiple rows of solid-color strips.

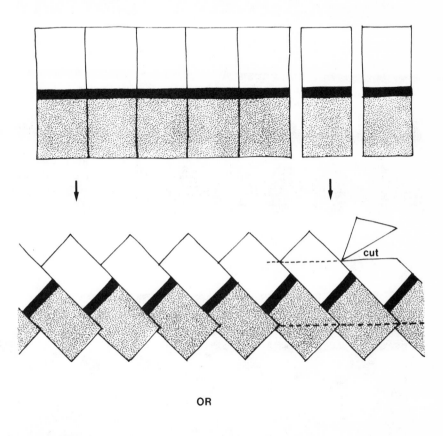

OR

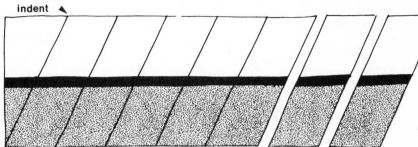

Figure C-1   *Seminole variations.*

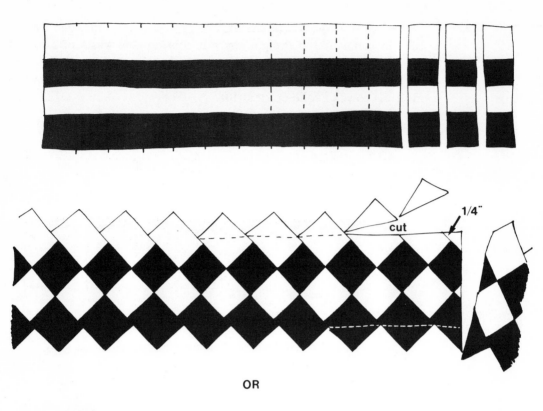

OR

Figure C-2 *Diamond and checkerboard variations.*

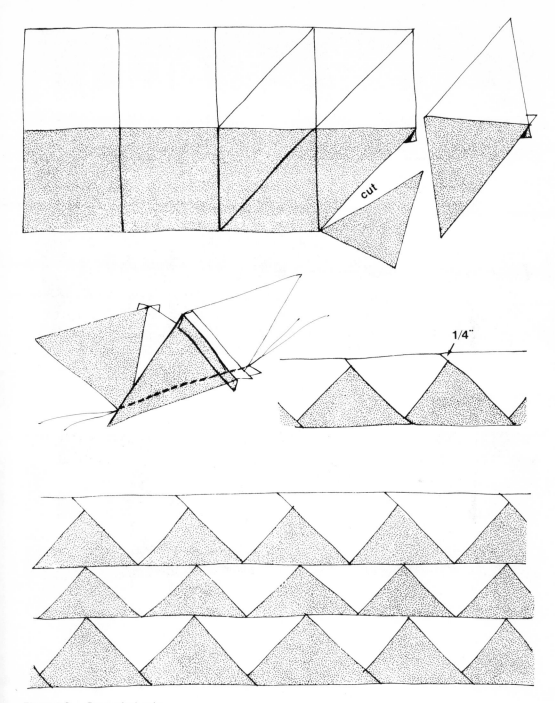

Figure C-3 *Rows of triangles.*

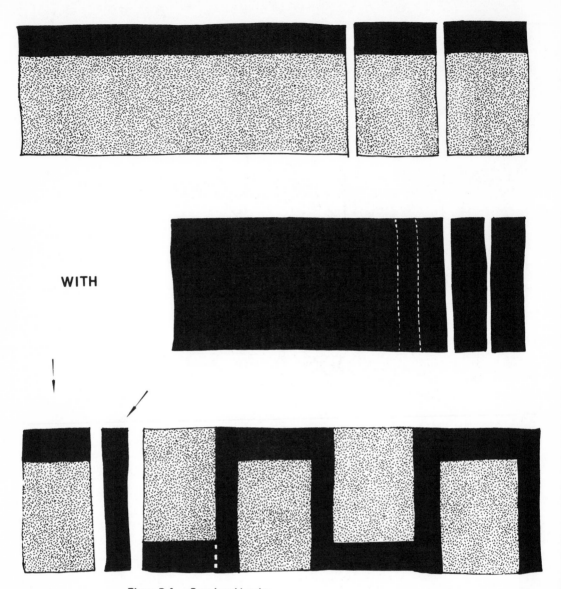

WITH

Figure C-4 *Bent band border.*

Examples of several Seminole-style patchwork pieces are shown in Figs. C-5 and C-6 and in Plates 20 and 21. The yokes and cuffs of the shirts are built into the garment, not topstitched onto a ready-made shirt.

Figure C-5   *Seminole-style patchwork hanging and pillow*, by the author, 1976.

· **Figure C-6**   *Seminole-style patchwork on shirt yoke*, by the author. Shirt by Judith James.

APPENDIX D: ON COLOR IN QUILTS

In the introduction to his book, *Interaction of Color*, Josef Albers states that ". . . color is the most relative medium in art." He makes the point that our perception of color is influenced by many external factors, not the least of which are the modifying effects that colors produce one relative to another.

This fact is of great importance to the quiltmaker. Unlike the painter or printmaker, the quiltmaker is rather restricted in his or her ability to physically manipulate color; it cannot be squeezed from a tube. Unless the quilter wishes to create painted or stained images directly on fabric, the physical demands of dyeing processes make this approach impractical. The quiltmaker's apparent color limitations, then, are set by the textile producers and by the exigencies of fashion. Throughout the traditional development of the craft, this has been so. However, the quilt artist who approaches color in fabric with serious intent and with an open and questioning attitude knows that those "apparent" limitations do not, in fact, restrict the expressive potential of the medium.

It is beyond the scope of this book to offer detailed analyses of color systems; a brief overview follows with references to works shown in the color plates. The serious quiltmaker, however, is directed to the section on color in the bibliography. Here will be found a selection of works dealing with the art of color that are worthy of further study.

One point should be kept in mind: the artist's application of color principles must at best include a large dose of imagination and creative judgment. Any conscious use of those color principles developed over the last three hundred years by color theorists, scientists, and artists, without allowance for subconscious (intuitive) responses to accidental or spontaneous color interactions, will give rise to no better than a static, anonymous surface. Color principles should be regarded as flexible and variable supports to the creative process.

TERMS

It's important to know what we're talking about. *Color* is, well, color—also called *hue* or *chroma*. It's what we perceive. *Value* is the relative lightness or darkness of a color. For example, pink is usually seen as a light value of red; maroon, on the other hand, is relatively dark in value. (See Nancy Crow's sensitive use of value gradations in the quilts shown in Plates 12 and 17.) Light values of a color are also called *tints*; if you were mixing pigment to achieve tint, you would add white to the pure color. For our purposes, the so-called pastel colors (pink, lime, peach, lavender, and so on) can be regarded as tints. Dark values of a color are called *shades*; they would result from the addition of black to the pure color. Navy, brown, maroon, Hunter green, and so forth, can be classified as shades. (Tints and shades contrast strikingly in "Medallion," Plates 19a and 19b.)

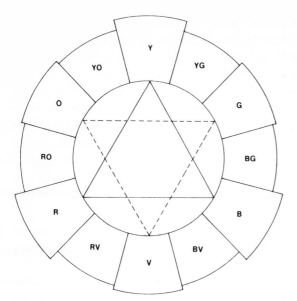

Figure D-1 *The Color Wheel.*
Clockwise from top, the colors are:
Yellow, Yellow-green, Green, Blue-green,
Blue, Blue-violet, Violet, Red-violet, Red,
Red-orange, Orange, Yellow-orange. At
the points of the solid triangle are the
primary colors, and at the points of the
dotted triangle are the secondary colors.

White and black mixtures produce values of gray, and gray mixed with pure color produces a *tone*. True tones in fabric are difficult to define unless one is able to see them in relation to other colors; however, beige, taupe, mauve, and khaki would likely be considered tones. Beige is seen as a light value, whereas khaki, by comparison, is a dark value.

Intensity is the strength or sharpness of a color—its saturation. It is the relative degree to which the color is pure or free of mixture with its complement and/or with white, black, or gray. The red in "Checquered Diamonds" (Plate 9) is nearly pure and displays a high degree of intensity.

THE COLOR WHEEL

The color wheel is the basic structure for ordering pure color. The one used most widely today contains the *primary* colors—yellow, blue, and red; the *secondary* colors—green, orange, and violet; and the *intermediate* colors—yellow-green, blue-violet, and red-orange; and red-violet, blue-green, and yellow-orange. Notice that each of these groupings forms an equilateral triangle on the color wheel. In and of itself, each grouping represents a distinct scheme of color harmony, however variable its appeal might be. Although you might hesitate to use pure green, pure orange, and pure violet together out of concern for the visual tug of war that might be created, a range of middle-to-light values of orange with a pale tint of green and two shades of purple could create an interesting color composition.

In "Dialogue" (Plates 16a and 16b) the artist uses a grouping of primary colors as a foundation for defining areas of color activity in the quilt. The richness of the color surface is a result of tonal variations within the three major chromatic areas.

Monochromatic arrangements are those that employ one color only, in a range of values of its tints, tones, and/or shades. The effect is generally one of complete unity. "Night Sky 2" (Plates 14a and 14b) is worked in a predominantly blue scheme; tension is created by the movement of the shapes and by the distinct light/dark contrasts.

Polychromatic arrangements exhibit a wide range of colors; the effect can be vividly exciting, much in the spirit of a celebration or carnival. Both "Florescent Rag" (Plate 10) and the parading "Menagerie" (Plate 11) derive their immediacy from the strong character of their polychromatic color schemes.

On the color wheel, *analogous* colors are groupings of any three adjacent colors. For example, red-orange, orange, and yellow-orange form an analogous harmony, as do blue-green, green, and yellow-green. Like monochromatic arrangements (of which these are slightly more complex variations), analogous harmonies usually effect an impression of unity and interrelatedness. A blue, blue-green, and green harmony is used as a foundation for ordering the colors in the Seminole-style patchwork shown in Plate 20.

Complementary colors lie in contrasting (opposite) positions on the color wheel. The complement of red is green; of blue it's orange, and of yellow-green it's red-violet. Complements appear to intensify one another. Green emphasizes the redness of red; violet intensifies the yellowness of yellow. A blue-green fabric can be made to appear more green than blue by placing it next to a strong red fabric; its blueness can be heightened by placing it with orange. When they are of equal or approximate value and intensity, adjoining complementary colors will effect startling "vibrations" at their edges. Depending on the context within which they are arranged, this can be either optically pleasing or disturbing. The color compositions in "Elaborated Tangram" (Plates 1a and 1b) and in "Incarnation" (Plate 17) draw on complementary contrasts for a large part of their visual power.

Split complementary harmonies involve any given color on the wheel and each of the colors adjacent to its complement. Red-violet, yellow, and blue-violet form a split complementary arrangement; likewise for orange, blue-violet, and yellow. This latter arrangement adds to the sense of excitement and activity captured in "Wicked Lily" (Plate 8).

It should be noted here that few if any of the quiltmakers whose work has been shown here actually sat down with a color wheel and deliberately plotted out a color scheme to be used in a given project. Although each has a working understanding of color principles, the choice of colors comes about through a gradual process of comparisons and eliminations by which intuitive responses to different color juxtapositions dictate the final fabric selection. However, when the artist wishes to effect a certain spirit or character or feeling in the quilt, a knowledge of how color works and of how particular viewer responses can be elicited will allow the quiltmaker to manipulate his or her collection of fabrics to its fullest expressive potential.

Bibliography

In each of the categories below, there are in print a greater number of excellent works than can be listed here. This selection catalogues a small number that, in the author's view, will best serve the needs of the serious quiltmaker.

HISTORY OF QUILTMAKING

Bishop, Robert. *New Discoveries in American Quilts.* New York: E. P. Dutton & Company, Inc., 1975.

———, and Elizabeth Safanda. *A Gallery of Amish Quilts.* New York: E. P. Dutton & Company, Inc., 1976.

Colby, Averil. *Patchwork.* London: B. T. Batsford Ltd., 1958.

———, *Quilting.* New York: Charles Scribner's Sons, 1971.

Haders, Phyllis. *Sunshine and Shadow*. New York: Universe Books, 1976.

Holstein, Jonathan. *The Pieced Quilt*. Greenwich, Connecticut: New York Graphic Society, Ltd., 1973.

Orlofsky, Patsy, and Myron Orlofsky. *Quilts in America*. New York: McGraw-Hill Book Company, 1974.

QUILT HOW-TO

Brown, Elsa. *Creative Quilting*. New York: Watson-Guptill Publications, 1975.

FitzRandolph, Mavis, and Florence M. Fletcher. *Quilting: Traditional Methods and Design*. Leicester: The Dryad Press, 1968.

Gutcheon, Beth. *The Perfect Patchwork Primer*. Baltimore: Penguin Books Inc., 1974.

Laury, Jean Ray. *Quilts and Coverlets: A Contemporary Approach*. New York: Van Nostrand Reinhold Company, 1970.

Newman, Thelma R. *Quilting, Patchwork, Appliqué, and Trapunto*. New York: Crown Publishers, Inc., 1974.

Short, Eirian. *Introducing Quilting*. New York: Charles Scribner's Sons, 1974.

TWO-DIMENSIONAL DESIGN

Bothwell, Dorr, and Marlys Frey. *Notan: The Dark-Light Principle of Design*. New York: Van Nostrand Reinhold Company, 1968.

Gutcheon, Beth, and Jeffrey Gutcheon. *The Quilt Design Workbook*. New York: Rawson Associates Publishers, Inc., 1976.

Justema, William. *The Pleasures of Pattern*. New York: Van Nostrand Reinhold Company, 1968.

Schoenfeld, Susan. *Pattern Design for Needlepoint and Patchwork*. New York: Van Nostrand Reinhold Company, 1974.

COLOR

Albers, Josef. *Interaction of Color.* New Haven: Yale University Press, 1971.

Birren, Faber. *Principles of Color.* New York: Van Nostrand Reinhold Company, 1969.

Itten, Johannes. *The Art of Color.* New York: Van Nostrand Reinhold Company, 1973.

Justema, William, and Doris Justema. *A Weaving and Needlecraft Color Course.* New York: Van Nostrand Reinhold Company, 1971.

ART/CRAFT IDEA

Albers, Anni. *On Designing.* Middletown, Connecticut: Wesleyan University Press, 1971.

Pye, David. *The Nature and Art of Workmanship.* New York: Van Nostrand Reinhold Company, 1971.

Richards, Mary Caroline. *Centering.* Middletown, Connecticut: Wesleyan University Press, 1962.

CATALOGUES

Bordes, Marilynn Johnson. *Twelve Great Quilts from the American Wing.* New York: The Metropolitan Museum of Art, 1974.

Burnham, Dorothy K. *Pieced Quilts of Ontario.* Toronto: Royal Ontario Museum, 1975.

DeGraw, Imelda G. *Quilts and Coverlets.* Denver: The Denver Art Museum, 1974.

Tanenhaus, Ruth Amdur. *The New American Quilt.* New York: Museum of Contemporary Crafts, 1976.

PERIODICALS

Canada Crafts, Page Publications Limited, 380 Wellington Street W., Toronto, Ontario M5V 9Z9.

Craft Horizons, American Crafts Council, 44 West 53rd Street, New York, New York 10019.

Fiberarts, 3717 4th N.W., Albuquerque, New Mexico 87107.

Quilter's Newsletter Magazine, Leman Publications, Inc., Box 394, Wheatridge, Colorado 80033.

Index